Once You Get Through the Mountains the Land Opens Up

Tecumshea S. Holmes, Sr.
P.O. Box 731
Edwardsville, IL 62025
TeckHolmes@aol.com
(618)530-8325

Once You Get Through the Mountains the Land Opens Up

Tecumshea S. Holmes, Sr.
B.S.S.S., M.Div., M.B.A.

Parkhurst Brothers Publishers
Marion, Michigan

www.parkhurstbrothers.com

Copies of this and other Parkhurst Brothers Publishers titles are available to organizations and corporations for purchase in quantity by contacting Special Sales Department at our home office location, listed on our web site. Manuscript submission guidelines for this publishing company are available at our web site.

Printed in the United States of America

First Edition, 2017

2017 2018 2019 2020 2021 2022 10 9 8 7 6 5 4 3 2 1

ISBN: Trade Paperback 978-1-62491-122-4

Parkhurst Brothers Publishers believes that the free and open exchange of ideas is essential for the maintenance of our freedoms. We support the First Amendment of the United States Constitution and encourage all citizens to study all sides of public policy questions, making up their own minds. Closed minds cost a society dearly.

The statements, assertions, conclusions and opinions expressed in this book are the work of the author exclusively.

Cover and interior design by	Linda D. Parkhurst, Ph.D.
Proofread by	Bill and Barbara Paddack
Acquired for Parkhurst Brothers Publishers by:	Ted Parkhurst

062017

Dedication

This work is dedicated to my wife, Kathleen, cousin Lanne, my brother Reginald J. Hampton, nephew Jeffery B. Hampton, my son Teck Money, daughters Tagwana, Kimberly and Talia, and grandchildren Madisen, Macy, Zach, and Harreld, III.

Table of Contents

Foreword

Greetings! As you look at this work prepared for you to read, you may wish to put it aside because to you it is just another book written by someone of little notoriety. But before you cast it aside, think about all the mountains that have stood before you. Remember, if you will, all of the mountains that kept you from your dreams, from your goals, and from your destiny. This little book is a device you and others such as yourself can read and use to conqueror your mountains.

When the book was begun, your writer looked back at his life, and he saw all the mountains that were placed before him. They turned into excuses as to why he had not accomplished as many feats, fame, riches, and acclaim as others around him. When he did an analysis of life, he determined that talent was not the thing he was missing. It was not hard work that denied him success. What held him back was not having the courage to become a mountain climber. From the time he was a child until recently, he had been raised in an environment that discouraged mountain climbing, metaphorically and literally. When he searched deeper into his past, he discovered that he had been conditioned to act and to react in a most conservative manner. This was his eureka moment! He discovered that all of his life up to this point was lived trying to conform to the expectations of others. He came to this pivotal moment and literally expunged from himself the breaks, road blocks, and impediments that stood before him.

The absence of all the specters of his past allowed this constrained creature to begin his ascension into the mountains. He put aside all the things that had weighed him down. He climbed the mountains. He saw from their peaks and the lands that lay opened before him. All he now needed to do was to descend from the mountains, and then decide in which direction he would travel the remainder of his life. He did just that, and he has been traveling across the open land. With this book, the author invites you to come down from the mountains, and travel the open lands. He now wants others to begin their climbs and their descents from the mountains. This book will aid you in climbing your mountains. It will help you as you climb down from your mountains, and it will guide you as you set off into the land that opens up.

Tecumshea S. Holmes, Sr.
B.S.S.S., M.Div., M.B.A.

Preface

LOOKING BACK OVER MY LIFE, I have seen some bad days, and I have seen some good days. When I added them all up, more of them have been good days. As we live and get older, things that upset us don't seem to matter as much anymore. Life brings with time a neutralizing effect. One does not sweat the little things that confronts him or her. I write this work to tell those who have not made it to this place that they need to know that the journeys we make in life have their share of mountains. And if they just continue climbing their mountains, things will get better. There are mountains we all confront, but when we get through them, the land opens up.

Mountains can be anything that seems to be insurmountable. They are the things that life places in our paths that stop us dead in our tracks. They are barriers that stand before us. They are there to keep us cut off from the other side. Your mountains might be coping with the diagnosis of cancer. Perhaps your life has been stopped with unbearable grief. Your beloved has died. Your dreams have turned into nightmares. Or you are struggling with addiction to legal or illegal substances. Crack is holding you back. Heroin has you locked down, or by no fault of your own, you got addicted to a prescribed opiate drug. Perhaps you are addicted to the one person who means you no good whatsoever. Mountains can be people who want to hold you back. They want to keep you where they are. And mountains can be the fear lodged deep within you. It tells you that you are nothing, you have never been anything, and you will never be anything. Take a moment and look at these mountains of yours. If your mountains are here, turn and look at them. They all have one thing in common. Mountains are sometimes beautiful, still, they are challenges we all face in life. They either make us or they break us. They stand between who we are and who we are meant by God to be.

Mountains are fates that want to deny us our destinies. The Creator's will is that we all should live abundant lives. Joy, peace and happiness (shalom) should be our constant companions. But our thoughts and actions get between His wishes for us. How do we return to the Lord's will for us? If you are not particularly religious, then how can you get better returns on your investments? We do this when we discover exactly what our personal mountains are. Once they are identified, we make plans that will enable us to overcome them. We climb them, and we make it through to the other side. When we arrive at the end of our trials, we know and understand where we have arrived and why we needed to be there. On the open plains, the rolling hills, the buttes, and mesas are new opportunities for you to decide to pursue. However, until you climb your mountains, you will never have the opportunities to enrich your lives.

As beautiful as the Appalachian and Smoky Mountains are, they were formidable impediments to be confronted and vanquished. If you are to live out your destinies, you cannot go any further until confrontations takes place. The crowd, the group, your circle of friends could be the foothills standing in your way. They remind you of how daunting the mountains are. They talk of the many dangers and difficulties that await you on your journey. They say things like this:

1. You have never done this before, stay here with us.
2. You don't have what it takes to make it through the mountains.
3. There are dangers associated with climbing mountains.
4. Fool, you don't even know what's on the other side of the mountains.
5. You need to be content with what you have.

All of these statements, and others like them, you have heard. The crowd never wants you to drop out and leave them. It is a threat to their existence, and they definitely are threats to your existence whether you realize it or not. If you are going to climb the mountains you have to drown out the voices of petrification. These voices are really stones, however so small, and over time they will weigh you down or they will wall you into your plight. You cannot, and you will not, even consider climbing your mountains as long as you listen to the crowd. Paul said in Hebrews 12:1, "… let us lay aside every weight and the sin that so easily ensnares us. Let us run with endurance the race that lies before us." This means you have to stop listening to the voices of the crowd. You have to let go of your doubts and your fears. You have to leave the places that you have become accustomed to in life. You must see yourselves as those who have been called out and who are destined for great journeys. Jesus said in Matthew 22:14, "For many are called, but few are chosen." He extends the invitation to individual perfection, and wholeness to any man or woman who will embark upon the quest of discovering what lies beyond the mountains. Sadly, few accept the invitation to begin the challenging journey. Why is this so? It is so because you find yourself in a quagmire or a predicament. To leave is to give up everything that you value. To stay is to give up those things that you might gain. Many of us are prisoners of our possessions.

Consider this, in India the people captured monkeys by drilling holes in staked-out coconuts and placing rice in the holes. The monkeys would place their hands inside the holes to retrieve the rice, but they could not withdraw their hands because they would need to open their hands. The monkeys would not leave the rice in order to free themselves. So after a few hours, the men would return to retrieve the staked-out monkeys. There are people who are staked out in similar situations. They cannot open their hands to receive the gifts and blessings life has given to them. You cannot receive these gifts with clenched fists. You have to open wide your hands to receive them. Are your fists open or are they closed? Do you want to forever be captive creatures of your fate? Are you willing to lose the world in order to gain your souls? (Matthew 16:26)

Beyond the mountains are the answers to why you were born. You will discover who you are and the gifts you bring to the world. Most importantly, you will find the peace (shalom) that has up to now eluded you. To get from here to there, you will need to silence the outside voices and the negative voices that have set up their homes inside of you. All around you there are legions of voices hell bent on keeping you in the ditches into which you have fallen. When you do these things, you will hear the still quiet voice of the Lord, guiding you along the pathways of your journeys (Psalm 119:105). There will be dangers seen and unseen on your travels, but you really have nothing to fear. David reminds us in Psalm 23:4 with these words, "Yea, though I walk through the valley of the shadow of death. I will fear no evil: for thou are with me; thy rod and thy staff they comfort me." What you need to remember is the same God who was with David is the same God who will be with you on your journeys. From personal experience I have come to know the Lord, and He is good. I know He cannot lie. His word was true when He told Moses and the Hebrew children in Deuteronomy 31:6, "Be strong and of a good courage, fear not, nor be afraid of them: for the Lord thy God, it is he that doth go with thee: he will not fail thee, nor forsake thee." Living and walking with Him beside you is a comfort. On your sojourning you have assurance better than Progressive's or Allstate's insurance. You just need to begin making your way towards the mountains. Don't allow anyone to turn you around!

The voices calling upon you to stay are the voices of the status quo. Move somewhere else so you cannot hear the voices of the herd. They exist to see to it that you remain on the seaward side of the mountains. They do not want you to fathom your thoughts about what exists on the other side of the mountains. They cannot bring themselves to wonder inwardly, let alone outwardly, about what there is to experience in the mountains or what lies beyond the mountains. If they cannot do this, they don't want you to do anything differently either. You and I know of people whom we graduated with from high school. We graduated, went away to college or university, and moved to where our new places of employment carried us. On occasions, we came back home to check on our parents or close relatives who stayed behind. When the word got out we were back, or we ran into them on the streets, their conversations were about what you and they did in bygone days. They seem to do this every time you meet them. How sad it is to be mentally trapped in a time warp. They are imprisoned in their past thoughts. They replay the same scenes over and over again, of days long past. You have experienced this in your lives, and like a cousin of mine, you may have decided not to go back there too often. Yes, reality tells you that was your home, but where you are now, is it your real home? Is it where you really should and need to be?

In truth you are the lucky ones because you left even when the crowd begged you not to leave. Some of you left the first girl or boy you fell in love with, to climb the mountains, and to see what lay on the other side of them. And there were some of you who wanted to leave desperately, and who needed to begin your journey, because the call was greater than the voices urging you to stay. If you have not made the move to leave, hopefully this will encourage you to strike out now. I feel your anxiety about leaving. Doing something entirely new and different is mind blowing. Let me share a recent experience with you. I went into the local Burger King where there was a young Black male. I spotted him immediately, partly because when I entered the place he stood up and gave me a welcoming smile. The others who were behind the counter barely gave me a passing glance. I gave him my order, and something prompted me to ask him about his studies. The young man told me he was attending Lewis and Clark Community College in town. I asked about his major, and he told me that he did not have a major. He went on to tell me that he knew nothing about college. He said he was the first person in his family to attend college. He also told me he was looking at business administration or business management as his major, but he wasn't good at math. I smiled at him and told him that business administration was the major that would offer him more opportunities. I assured him that he could conquer the math by going to the college's math tutoring lab, studying hard, and by believing in himself. And I told him that if he worked hard, in the end he could make a six-figure income. And I cautioned him about majoring in business management. So many Black college and university students are sidetracked into this field of study.

It is like when I was attending university, we were encouraged by the guidance counselor to become teachers, psychologists or sociologists. These were low-paying, helping fields that saw us working hard and falling behind economically. I want you to know that you cannot help others until you can help yourself. You do not do anyone any service being in the ditch with them. It is only when you can reach down and pull them out of the ditches that you are helping them. To the young man at the restaurant I stressed the limitations for advancement in corporate America by majoring in business management, and should he want to become an entrepreneur, the risks and rewards. I told him that a bachelor's degree in business administration would equip him to work in any field of business he selected, including human resources, marketing, finance, communications, and accounting. I also told him about being so fortunate to live in the town where one of the nation's top tiered businesses schools was located. He looked puzzled. I shared with him that Southern Illinois University at Edwardsville was accredited with the same accreditations held by Harvard, Princeton, and Yale Universities. I told him that I would love to help him along the way. I gave him my business card and told him not to hesitate to call me when he needed directions or clarification. I took my order and left. What stuck in my mind was that there are so many young men and women like him. They are striking out to climb their mountains. Some have guides to help them, but other climbers have no one to help them as they begin their ascents into the mountains. I pray and hope that if you have made it through the mountains, and you encounter those who are starting to climb their mountains, that you will lend them as much aide as possible.

Some who begin the journey turn back because they do not have a guide to aid them. When things got difficult for them, they did not have an assuring voice to steady their nerves, and to tell them that lesser men and women have made the crossing. This is the problem within the Black community. So many uninformed and inexperienced men and women turn back prematurely because there were no voices of encouragement. They needed mentoring and role models so they could see that the journey and the climb were possible. Black America will not take its place among the decision makers as long as those who have climbed the mountains refuse to leave trail makers for others to follow. Enough said about this. Let us continue preparing for our mountains.

Take a look at the mountains. There is one that will become your personal Everest. And when you realize which peak is your personal challenge to conquer, remember the late Sir Edmund Hillary and his guide Tenzing Norgay. The year was 1953. Before these two men stood the god of all mountains—Everest, the tallest mountain in the world. All other mountains held court around its summit. Many men tried to reach its peak, but they died trying or they turned back in defeat. Sir Hillary and Tenzing were aware of the formidable challenge, the awe, and danger that stood before them. In my mind's eye I can hear the voices of the people begging them not to assault the mountain. They talked about the many who died attempting to climb Everest. They pleaded with the two men to let the King of Mountains be. But the two men knew instinctively that they were men of destiny. They were aware of the many who died before them. They also knew according to the odds, they would not make it. They also knew that playing the odds did not allow for risk taking. Discoveries have been made by those who dared to risk. Fortunes have been acquired because some men and women wagered it all for that one sure opportunity. Listen! No one who has ever become successful, and at peace with themselves, took the odds seriously. The odds are mathematical probabilities that figure out the chances of your winning or accomplishing things. Odds are fates working to keep you average. But you are not average. You are exceptionally made. You are part of a royal priesthood. Don't let the odds even enter your thoughts. The odds place mental barriers and limits on your dreams and aspirations. Every child of the Lord is not ordinary. If you are a child of the King, then you are not average, and you are not limited by your present situations or circumstances.

Joseph went through a series of disappointments and setbacks in his life. His older brothers became jealous of him. They conspired together and sold him into slavery in Egypt. Joseph may well have been heartbroken at his brothers' action, but he kept his wits about himself. He was sold to Potiphar, the captain of the guard in the service of Pharaoh. He did not make the mistake of just being another slave. He worked diligently, and his work was exceptional. Soon Joseph became the overseer of the House of Potiphar. This is what exceptionalism does for you. However, Potiphar's wife noticed this in Joseph. He was young, good looking, and he was extremely intelligent. She propositioned Joseph not once, but on many occasions. It just so happens that on one occasion too many, she came onto him so strongly that the young man had to leave his garment as he fled from her. Potiphar's wife was enraged. The Bible says she held onto Joseph's garment, and when her husband came home, she accused Joseph of trying to assault her. The Bible tells us in Proverbs 8:5 that, "Hell hath no fury like a woman scorned!" This woman was angry and outdone. She was seething with rage, and she wanted revenge.

Potiphar had Joseph imprisoned for her accusations. An average person would have gone to pieces. But Joseph knew that the Lord did not bring him that far to leave him.

Not many young men run into women like this man's wife. And if they do and find themselves in trouble, they need to know that their present circumstances will not last long. Life has shown me that a lie will have gone halfway around the world before truth sets its foot outside of the door. But as Martin Luther King, Jr., said, quoting William Cullen Bryant, "Truth crushed to earth will rise again." Joseph was lied about and subjected to the harsh anger of his master's wrath, but he instinctively knew that the Lord can open a door that no man or woman can close. What your enemies see as prisons to confine you are actually rooms of preparation for you. The lad went into prison knowing that trouble would not last always. When you are exceptional, you know even when you cannot see a solution to your predicament that the Lord will see you through to the other side.

In prison the Lord was with Joseph, and he softened the heart of the chief jailer. The jailer showed favor to Joseph. Even in prison, Joseph's exceptionalism was on display. He became the prison's "turnkey." He was the chief administrator of his prison, answerable only to the chief jailer. When you walk by faith, and not by sight, the Lord will exalt you higher than the mountains of your circumstances. The scriptures tell us that, "… all things work together for good to them that love God, to them who are the called according to his purpose" (Romans 8:28). In this story found in Genesis chapters 37-48, Joseph's downfalls were preludes to his uprisings. He was given by the Lord the ability to interpret dreams. One faithful day Joseph interpreted the dreams of Pharaoh's butler and baker. He told the men that within three days Pharaoh would lift up the head of the butler and restore him to his position. He then told the baker that during that same time Pharaoh would lift up his head, but he would be hung on a tree. These things came to pass, but as true as they were nothing immediately came of it for Joseph. He continued to languish in prison. As your troubles stand as mountains before you, don't get disappointed if the Lord does not move them from before you right away. You see, he wants you to climb over whatever your conditions may be at the time. Know that the Lord weaves the fabric of time to sew your garments of exaltation. Also, you should know that you can't hurry or rush the Lord in making for you a way out of no way. If you just wait in anticipation, the door of freedom will open for you. If you silently wait on him, in due time, your deliverance will come.

Joseph carried on his work, and he did not give up on the promises of the Lord. God cannot lie, and He does not lie. His Word opens doors that no man can close. His Word closes doors that no man can open. In prison the chief jailer did not acknowledge Joseph's abilities to interpret dreams. He did not tell anyone in the palace above his station about Joseph. But like a light in a dark room, its rays will pierce the darkness and shine through. Pharaoh had been troubled by a series of dreams he was having. His priests, magicians, and wise men could not interpret the troubling dreams. Then and only then, at the right time and at the right place, the butler remembered Joseph. He told Pharaoh about what Joseph had told him, and how those things came to pass. Pharaoh immediately sent for Joseph. And Joseph told Pharaoh what his dreams meant. Joseph told Pharaoh that there would be seven years of plenty followed immediately by seven years of famine in the land. The words of Joseph assured Pharaoh. From that moment on, there was no more troubling of Pharaoh's mind. He believed Joseph's interpretation, and he appointed Joseph as administrator over the preparations of the coming famine. With his new station Joseph set up granaries throughout the kingdom to store grain for the lean times.

You may be surrounded by problems that are higher than the height at which you stand. But do not worry yourself because the Lord is still in the exalting business. You will always be able to rise higher than the mountain of troubles that seem to have you hemmed in—with no way out. You and I could go on with this story, but it just shows what a child of God can do, and what he or she can become in life. Climbing mountains sometimes takes you into a deep gorge, but if you keep climbing, you will make your way up and out of it.

Now, let's return to see how Mount Everest was climbed. The two men began the ascent of the King of Mountains slowly, measuring each track they left in the snow. There were dangerous incidents, but still they went forward. They passed through howling winds, frigid cold, and thinning oxygen levels. Finally, after 8,850 meters, the two men reached the summit of Mount Everest. The mountain had been conquered. Together, they stood at the top of the world. Their gazes looked at sights that eyes had never seen previously. The mountain had been subdued. You and I need to remember that there is nothing too hard for God. When you are faced with what looks to be beyond your capacity alone, you need to call upon the Lord for His guidance. He will see you through. Your mountain awaits you. You too can domesticate your greatest challenges by relying on the Almighty and believing you have what it takes. The Lord takes ordinary people and he does extraordinary things with them. If you take your Bible and leaf through the pages, you will see how the Lord took nobodies and used them to stand against giants. He used them to walk through fiery furnaces and not be burned. He used them to play with furious lions as if they were common kitty cats. When you become pliable in the hands of God, He will transform you into an amazing person.

Sir Hillary and Tenzing Norgay only climbed one mountain. That mountain was the one that no man or woman had conquered up to then. The Lord left it there for these two men to subdue. You must climb many mountains and be faced with the dangers like they were presented. However, any man or woman who leaves those who would hold them back and begins their tracks will make it through the mountains. Yes, in the mountains there are peaks and there are valleys. There are falling boulders. There are crevices and sudden snowstorms to test you. But tests show you what you have learned, and what you need to study harder in order to pass the next test. Every great man or woman has had to climb his or her mountain. Never does life shower its riches on the ordinary. The average, they stay average. The bold, intrepid ones use their mountain experiences to perfect their minds as well as their bodies for what awaits them on the other side.

Mountain ranges may be high and vast, but they do not go on forever. A missed opportunity becomes a specter that haunts your waking hours and it goes on into your sleepless nights. It writes your epitaph: *"Failure by failing to accomplish anything."* You see, there are those among us who can't do anything right. They fail to grasp the prize awaiting them on the other side of the mountains. They fail at seeing the opportunities that are before them. They fail at overcoming the fear that consumed their lives. Where there is fear there is no faith, no hope, and no peace of mind. What is so sad is these poor souls fail at living life itself. There are those who exist, and there are those who live life. If you get nothing else from this work, remember life is short, but it still demands that we live. What time the three sisters of fate have allotted to us, we need to live to the fullest.

Look at the inner cities of America. Here you see those who began the journey through the mountains, but they became prisoners of the mountains. They are captives of drug addiction, unemployment, gang violence, police brutality, and despair. They began their journeys as migrants of the 1929 Great Depression. Some came during World War II as workers in the military armament factories to bolster the war efforts. And there were others who fled the burning crosses and the hangings of the Ku Klux Klan in the Jim Crow southern states during the 1920s, 1930s, 1940s, 1950s, 1960s, and 1970s. Where these poor souls made their mistakes, was to mistake the mountains for their final destinations. The mountains were transitory passages from where they came from, to where they were, and where they were ultimately supposed to lead them to the end of their journeys.

They are sort of like the older people who left Egypt with Moses. They did not go into the Promised Land because they were forbidden to enter into it. They turned a few days journey into a forty-year pilgrimage. To them, leaving Egypt was the end-all accomplishment. They could not get their thoughts around going a little further. If they had just continued their sojourning, they would have entered the Promised Land. Like the Israelites who got manna from heaven to eat, Blacks who left the South got more than they ever had. However, they were still just inside of the mountains. Post-Reconstruction Blacks did not even know or understand this.

You might not know this, but in the mountains there are valleys where crops can be grown. There are sheep, bears, snow leopards, fowl, and other animals inhabiting the mountains. There are enough substances within the mountain valleys for cities to arise, and where people can band together to become clans and nations. Look at your globes and your maps of the world. High up in the Himalayas are the nations of Nepal, China, India, Pakistan, Afghanistan, and Bhutan. These are ancient lands that are thousands of years old. So this makes my point, as hostile as mountains look, they yield nourishment to those who know where to find it. Those who wandered for forty years in the wilderness lived, ate, and went about their business until the last of them died. They were trapped by their ambitions of just getting by.

As for the urban centers of America, there are slums and ghettos where millions of men and women are not living; they are just surviving. In the urban centers of America there are at least five generations of those who have made the valleys of plight their homes. They have been wandering in the slums longer than the Hebrew children wandered in the wilderness. As good as Section Eight Housing and the Link Cards are, they are not substitutes for what awaits you on the other side of the mountains. The Hebrew children lived in tents during the forty years of wandering. The urban centers where millions of Blacks reside aren't even theirs to own. And the ones who have titles of ownership are living in houses that are the fruition of other people's dreams. When are Black Americans going to stop paying top dollars for other people's left behinds?

When my wife and I decided to move to Edwardsville, Illinois, we had our differences. She wanted to look at houses that were previously owned. But I insisted that we look at houses that were newly built. I finally got her to listen to me, and one day she was persuaded to look at a house I had fallen in love with just a few doors down from where one of my nieces lived. She hated the outside appearance of the house but agreed to take a walk through anyway. Our Realtor met us outside, and we went inside. Immediately, I was astonished when she saw the kitchen layout. She exclaimed, "I'll take it!" Inside the ugly house was now just what she was looking for. More important to me was the fact that everything in it was brand new. What we saw there was an open floor plan we could make our own. And this we did together. We have lived in the house for more than ten years. During these years there have been some renovations, but every stud and nail adding change are our own, and not someone else's. Together, the wife and I left behind the hills of Alton, Illinois, and we settled on the plains of Edwardsville, Illinois. In a sense, the land opened up for us.

When Moses sent his spies into the Promised Land, they returned with a cornucopia of food. They reported to the people that the land was full of riches. They described it as the Land of Milk and Honey (Exodus 33:3), and under Joshua they entered into it. If you are one who is still in the mountains, know that on the other side of the mountains you will find your Promised Land. You will not have to worry about drive-by shootings. You can rest at night because your neighbors are not blaring their music as loud as it gets. You can walk to the supermarket and purchase nourishing food at reasonable prices. You can live where you want to live and not where Section Eight allows you to live. For more than seven generations you have been living mostly on handouts. On the other side of the mountains you can live on the blessings of what the Lord (YHWH) has set aside especially for you and you alone. If you have lost your vision, you can call upon the Lord to renew your spirit and to give you an upright heart. The new you will compel you to move beyond the valleys and the mountains. Your renewed journey will carry you to the place where the land opens up.

Going into the mountain range, you will find yourselves going higher and higher as the elevations take you to the highest peaks. Now you find yourselves moving downward on the mountains. You come to see that the prizes that beckoned you onward are before you. Your pace quickens. Still, you use caution as you make you way off the mountains. You have come too far to fail now. You see sights never before seen. You can view the plains that call you onward. On your way down, periodically stop and see what lies before you on the land below.

It is here that your final destinations should be contemplated. When you look at a mountain range, you will see that in the middle of the range the mountains are highest. On the outer sides of the mountains, descending is like stepping down. Going in, you step up and up. Coming down, you step down, down until you are on smooth ground. What begins on your journeys is a more difficult ascent, and what ends is a less tiring descent. So often, people go through the mountains as if getting through them is their where-withal. The mountains are your journeys, your testing grounds, and they are where you contemplate on who you were and who you and the Lord want you to become. You have seen celebrities who at some point in their careers suddenly stop and drop out of society. Or they descend into destructive behavior. They were in such a rush to make it off the mountains that they neglected to determine who they were to become. They did not find out what they were to do on the other side. Our entire lives have to be lived with our eyes open and focused on what lies before us. We cannot go back to the past. All we have is the present, and the hope of what tomorrow will bring. While we are in the now moment of time, we must adjust or focus to keep on the pathways and to decide where we will go when we get there. Do this while you are still walking towards your destinations. In just a few more labored steps we will have made it to where the land opens up.

If you climbed higher than you have ever climbed before, you have conquered your mountains. Now you find yourself exhausted, cut, and bloodied by the jagged outcroppings of the mountains, but you made it through. Perhaps you are so beaten up by your tedious journeys that you cannot think. You are just in the moment of being on the other side of the Goliaths behind you. But I ask you to pull it all together and give me your attention. I want you to look at the land that is before you. It is filled with opportunities you cannot fathom. As it is said, "What does not kill me [you], will make me [you] stronger" (Friedrich Nietzsche, *Twilight of the Idols*, 1888). Having been so close to your mortal deaths you have acquired insights that few men or women have. You have been given resources, now use them wisely. You ask, what does this mean? You have seen the void of death, and you have lived to tell about it. There is nothing else you need to fear. You know now that one's thoughts when pursued become realities. Now as you go into the land that is opened up before you, follow the visions, and the dreams that lie within you. Your dreams have the power now to become living matter, things, institutions, and corporations—anything that is an extension of you.

Here is what I am trying to tell you. Guglielmo Giovanni Maria Marconi went to sleep one night and in his dream the entire schematic to the wireless radio was given to him. It was as if the universe itself revealed this to him. Upon awaking he immediately began construction of the first working, practical wireless radio. Then there was a Black American inventor named Elijah McCoy who lived during the "Jim Crow" era of American history. Elijah did not allow the confinements of racism to hold him back. He invented the oil-drip cup that greatly aided the railroad industry. And before him, there was Booker T. Washington. He was born a slave in Virginia. His father was most likely the man who owned his mother and him. Booker T. did not go into the re-enslavement system of sharecropping, but instead he went to Hampton Institute in Virginia and acquired an education. He wanted to free others like himself, including Native Americans. He went on to establish, on the wings of a prayer, Tuskegee University in 1881.

He also, unknowingly, laid the foundation for the training of Black American airmen who served and fought with honor and distinction during World War II. For it was at Tuskegee University that the Black pilots were taught how to fly airplanes. These pilots went on to distinguish themselves dog fighting over the skies of North Africa and Europe. Oh yes, and let us not forget the soldiers who served and fought against the Confederacy, and against unequal pay in the Union Army in which they served. They declined this injustice, and they let their unequal pay lay. Their prorated wages as soldiers piled up, and over time it appreciated into a tidy sum. After the end of the Civil War, they took their refused pay and used it to establish Lincoln University in Jefferson City, Missouri. Finally, we should remember a wirily girl from East St. Louis, Illinois, who left home for Europe as a teenager during the Roaring Twenties. She was a nothing here in America, but in Paris she was an instant sensation. She educated herself and became the belle of France. This woman placed her life on the line as a member of the French Underground. She adopted children from around the world. She showed Black American women who came after her that dreams do become realities. She was Josephine Baker. You get the drift by now? There are dreams and visions within you that are waiting to become realities.

Have courage and take heart as you set your feet onto the land. Inherit the land, build on the land. Multiply and make the world better than you found it. Laugh more than you cry. Love yourself as much as you love someone else. Forgive and you too will be forgiven. Give as much as you receive. Find time to commune with the God of the universe. And don't take life or yourselves too seriously. The land, it is good land. Should your mountains be personal in nature take heart and have courage. Move through them until you get to the land.

Your doctor has come into the examining room with a troubled look on his or her face. You immediately begin worrying about what will come out of his or her mouth. Your doctor looks sternly into your eyes and gives you really terrible news. You have cancer, not just any cancer, but a rapidly progressive form of cancer. You are told by your doctor that you have less than six months to live. Your heart sinks, and you are crying uncontrollably. You ask if there could be a mistake in the tests run on you. The reply is a definite no! Your doctor and his nurse try to comfort you, but you cannot be consoled. You ask why, you plead with God, and you finally get it together to walk out of your doctor's office and towards your car. This is now the mountain you must climb. You have been given one of two choices. You can accept the prognosis of your doctor, or you can make up your mind to either beat the cancer, or to live beyond the date of the death sentence given to you. Life has a way of bringing mountains to you. You find yourself between the coast and the other side of the mountains. You have one of two choices to make. You can remain on the coast and be hemmed in by sorrow and by those who offer words of comfort as they wait for you to die. Or you can look inward or heavenward to gather the last remaining strength within yourself.

With this final reserve of strength, energy, and power, you

begin climbing your mountains. Your climbing tools are not ropes, hooks, and picks. Instead of these you use your God, or whatever belief system you have, to carry you through. If you are not a religious person, you look inward and somehow you pull from the inner most part of your being the will to live fully until you chose to die. You take this attitude and strike out towards your mountains. The person of faith uses his or her God to begin and end the journey. The person of indomitable will uses the will to live, until he or she decides to die. Both of these individuals know that life, in situations such as these, ends when they call time. As a former chaplain, I have seen people linger outside of death's door until they decide, or they are given permission, to enter within. There was a member of one of the parishes I pastored. Mr. Washington was his name. He had a massive stroke, and was semi-conscious when I entered the emergency room where he lay. The monitor showing his vitals would hover close to death, but when his wife would call out to him to stay, his vital signs would rally, and he would gain strength from God knows where. I watched him labor for the better part of half an hour, then I asked his wife to give him permission to go on through the door. She was resistant to doing this because she wouldn't have anyone to wait on her hand and foot. I told her he was suffering and wanted her permission to die. Reluctantly she relented, and she and I both told Mr. Washington to go on toward the light. Immediately his breathing became less labored, and a smile appeared across his face. He left this side of life and entered the other side, within a minute of being told it was all right for him to die. Mr. Washington's mountains were the unreasonable expectations of his wife. When he was freed from them he saw something that brought a smile upon his face. I was convinced that there is something beyond this life after witnessing what took place in that room. Sometimes people climb mountains that permit them to tie up loose ends. They cannot die until they have seen home or loved ones for the last time. They will not die until they have made recompense for a slight they had done in the past. These and other mountains like them must be crossed before the Promised Land opens up before them.

Then there are those who are substance abusers who come to the "ah ha" moments where they see those on the coastal side of the mountains dying daily around them. They see the coast as certain death for them, and within them is the strong will to do more than just survive. They want to live. In making this decision a person looks at the mountains as a better choice. They climb the peaks, and they climb the valleys one day at a time. They climb their mountains one minute, one second, one prayer, and one hope at a time. But as hard and as difficult as it is they know, that like their addictions, this thing has its beginning and ending. They have come to realize that the pain and suffering they have experienced, and will experience, will not last always. They know that life is not just existing; it is living through hope. Hope is the seed which when planted and watered with tears turns into faith. Nothing we accomplish in life comes without tears of frustration, tears of pain, and tears of suffering. I remember watching my children being born. I stood by the sides of their mothers who endured the birthing pains while tears flowed. I saw their brows wet with sweat as they strained to bring new life into this world. But when they made the final push, and the children came into this world, screaming and covered in the birthing fluids, my wives excitedly smiled and offered tears of joy. It is like this with the men and women who are tired of being tired. They are fed up with living each day more dead than alive. They have resolved to move away from the coast and up into the mountains and on through to their recoveries. They know unconsciously that the land opens up on the other side.

Perhaps you or someone you know is living in an unfulfilling marriage or relationship. They are as addictive to this suffering as a crack addict. They want to leave the relationship, but they persuade themselves that they must remain there for the sake of the children. They tell themselves they cannot make it alone. They listen to outside voices that pile guilt upon them, whenever they come close to moving on with their lives. All of these excuses are as flimsy as one strand of cotton thread. These individuals are prisoners of self-doubting. The only things holding them there are themselves. Suddenly they have the presence of mind to leave. They just open their eyes, and they see things differently. They understand that no time will ever be the right time to leave. They get it! They know it is time to leave because life is too short to waste, living with someone who does not love you, and who you don't love. They may have seen on the six o'clock news a story of how refugees from Syria or Iraq came to this country with nothing but the clothes on their backs. Now they are prospering in their newly adopted homeland. They look at the news story, and they resolve to do likewise. They see that their mountains are not as high, or as long to get through. They just need to leave, to move on, and to move out. Yes, there will be adjustments, but these adjustments should have been made a long time ago. The children will notice the changes in them and they will change, too. The partners left behind will finally be able to discover who they are. They may even find others who bring them the joy and happiness you never could. They have made life so much better for others as well as for themselves. It may be they are experiencing living for the first time.

Again, as living beings, we need to constantly remember that life is finite in this plain of existence. Neither you nor I have seen what exists beyond this present moment. All we have is the time that blood runs warm through our veins. This is where we seek out our individual destinies. Our fortunes and our fates are predetermined by the mountains we choose to conqueror, or not to conqueror. Who we are and who we will become, is dependent upon whether we stay where we are, or whether we journey through the mountains; to get to where the land opens up.

 *Readers Notes*

Some Completed their Journeys Others Returned

THERE ARE MANY PEOPLE WHO HAVE MADE THEIR PERSONAL JOURNEYS through their mountains. Making it through the mountains were mind and thought-altering experiences for those who made it to the other side. They learned that the world is larger than the small communities from whence they came. The men and women who began their journeys learned that they possessed more strength and fortitude than they realized. Each of these individuals discovered that deep within their unconscious minds were replenishing streams of determination. They also discovered, on the other side, that they were not alone, but that they were parts of a greater fraternity of seekers. Each man and woman blazed trails of knowledge, learning, and discovery that has and is advancing society even today. President Barack Obama, Steve Jobs, Bill and Hillary Clinton, Thomas Edison, Madame Marie Curie, Mahatma Gandhi, and a host of others have brought new lights into this world. They have made great advances that are benefitting the whole of society. Each of these individuals came down from the mountains, with new purposes to seek in life. They left behind the collective minds that were like the Borgs of Star Trek fame. They did not want to be assimilated into the collective.

Here, on the other side of the mountains, each one of them has to determine his or her personal destiny, raison d'etre, and purpose in life. Back on the far side of the mountains life would have ended for them, not knowing who they were. Still, as great a reward as self-actualization is, there are some who complete the journey to the other side of the mountains only to immediately turn around and return to the mundane existences of their old lives. Each returnee is outer-directed. Each of them is afraid to look within to learn who he or she is. So they return to the other side of the mountains and live out their days just like they had lived in the past. The returnees are the heroes as described by Joseph Campbell. The heroes Campbell described, in his work entitled *The Hero With a Thousand Faces* return to their points of origin not because they are afraid of what lay ahead. They returned to share with those left behind new thoughts and new ways of looking at life. Each hero brought back to his or her home new possibilities of interacting with others and one's self. They carry back to those left on the other side of the mountains, "boons" or divine gifts of knowledge, insights, and spirituality. Unfortunately, most of these returning heroes are killed or destroyed by the people to which they bring words of new ideas, knowledge, and truths.

This is what happened to Jesus. It is what happened to Moses as well. He led the Hebrew people out of Egyptian captivity and all the way to the banks of the Jordan River. Except, he himself did not enter into the Promised Land. Moses could only view the Promised Land while he saw the Hebrew people entering the land. There are high probabilities that to return to the other side of the mountains will be more injurious to those returning, than their being accepted with elation and growth from those still on the other side of the mountains. This is because the majority of the people left behind have closed minds. They have eyes that cannot see. And they have ears that cannot hear (Mark 18:10).

Many of you who are considering going all the way back to where you started from need to reconsider what you are thinking. I have come to realize that you can't change stupidity or insanity. One will leave you utterly frustrated, and the other will literally kill you. Those left behind have closed their eyes and minds to new things. They are like the Flat Earth Society who to this day refuse to believe the world is a sphere. The society's founder, Samuel Shenton, converted thousands of people to repudiate scientific evidence proving the world is more like the shape of a ball.

History is full of people who returned home, only to perish at the hands of those they sought to assist. They described what they found in the open land and what exists in the mountains, but the people did not believe them. Those in control could not allow the returnees to live. The thought masters did not want the returnees spreading their new ideas and thoughts among the masses over which they long held control.

Sometimes it is the masses themselves who reject outright the news brought back by the returnees. The masses are so conditioned to think narrowly until they believe the returnees to be fools. You need to remember you can only feed a person who is hungry new dishes. You can only motivate or change people who find themselves in catastrophic danger. And even in situations such as this, you will only get a handful of the people to believe you. Remember, a prophet is not without honor except in his own hometown (Matthew 13:57). A case in point, climate change is melting the ice that closed off the Arctic. Now cruise lines are booking passengers to see and explore this region that had been inaccessible. Every time there is an appreciable amount of rainfall in Florida and Louisiana, there is massive flooding. In Alaska entire villages are being forced to relocate further and further inland. The Bering Sea is encroaching as the permafrost turns the ground to muddy mush. And yet there are people who deny the science and the signs. They continue to pollute and to build luxury condominiums on the coastal edges of the oceans. When will they learn that they cannot rebuild the coastlines faster than the oceans are tearing them down?

Going back is a losing proposition to anyone who returns to where he or she came from. It is in your best interest to go into the open land. There you can recreate yourselves. In this new place you can build arks to preserve the best of humanity to the right and to the left of you. Look at what now awaits you. There are more possibilities than you could ever imagine ahead of you. Here is where you need to wait and give thoughtful consideration as to where you will go and what kind of life you will make in this new land. This is because so many have struggled through the mountains only to be lost and destroyed by the vast opportunities that are before them.

Lamar Odom, the professional basketball player who married one of the Kardashian women, failed to do what I am suggesting. Now the world watches the news for information about his struggle for life. This man was stricken with what appears to be a stroke. He had been partying at a Nevada brothel for several days. During this time he was taking excessive amounts of drugs. He appears to be like so many others who have struggled to get to the big times, only to fall apart once they have arrived. So many actors and professional athletes spend all their money and lose their pro contracts in rapid succession. M.C. Hammer did this. Toni Braxton did this also. They failed to plan for the time they would enter onto the open land.

My son, whom I love dearly, is another prime example of this factor. He was selected for the MTV show entitled the Real World. He was one of the cast members who went to Hawaii. He developed an appreciable following, and after the series ended he was in great demand. He starred in an MTV movie and had small parts in a few more. He was even given two or three shows with MTV. The last project he had was being the host of the Cartoon Network's Hole in the Wall. Then, just as sudden as his rise, there was his descent. Presently he gets a part here and there but nothing like before. What I am saying to you is, once you see the new land for the first time, come up with several plans to fall back upon, if and when they become necessary.

Wasn't it Andy Warhol who said everyone will get his or her fifteen minutes of fame? I sure had my fifteen minutes of fame when my wife and I were guests on one of the Real World Hawaii episodes. But when that was over, I returned to the St. Louis metropolitan area and went back to teaching. I also finished my MBA program and used what I learned from the program to develop a modest retirement portfolio. I am not rich, but knowing my two percent Social Security cost of living increase isn't happening does not affect my standard of living. You should remember that you planned before you assaulted the mountains. You need to plan in which direction you will go now that you are on the open land. Be it to the left or the right, you still must plan for any and all contingencies. If you keep going straight ahead, you still need to plan and map out your route. After crossing the mountains, those who planned were successful. Planning did not suddenly stop once they came down from the mountains. Planning involves deciding things. What are your objectives and what are your ultimate goals? What is the allocated time limit for acquiring such?

Success does not remain with the lucky for long, but it does spend a long time with those who have planned. With this in mind, as you survey the openness, decide what your plans are now.

In case you didn't notice it there are many others just like you. They too have made it through the mountains. Please be careful here, the others may have come together and may beforming themselves into an aggregation or large mass. You should not be so quick to become a part of the group. Remember on the other side of the mountains, it was the voices of the group telling you to stay with them. You need to understand that the herd mentality is what makes you average. You made it through the mountains alone with wit, faith, and great effort. You became an exceptional individual, so why put yourself back to being average? As I see it, your future success in the open land is predicated upon your standing out as unique and appealingly different. People who are different have their own brands of charisma that no one else has. Take what you have been given and use it to further your plans. Please, for goodness sake, don't waste it on the undeserving. There will always be those who will seduce the weak minded and like wraiths or ghosts drain them of their uniqueness and creativity. My advice here is to keep your eyes on your goals. Way too many exceptional men and women have crossed their mountains only to lose their sense of self. Drugs have destroyed so many who went into the open lands without plans. They failed to make a difference in this world. They did not make a difference because they could not understand the gifts they possessed. Not only they, but you and I where ever we might be, can make a difference in this world. We all come with limits, but despite our limits each and every one of us can make unlimited changes for the better.

Remember what I am about to share with you about allowing

others to drain away your uniqueness. There are many types who are dangerous, but I will share with you the ones who are more adept at draining the gifted and the unique. There are those who appear needy and helpless, and they invoke the tender side within nearly all of us. However, these people are enchanters who are lions waiting to ensnare the unsuspecting. Samson fell to Delilah because she used some of the tricks of the trade on him. She got him so wrapped up in her agenda that he forgot that he was to be a champion and savior for Israel against the Philistines. Delilah drained Samson of his strength and his will to be a savior for his people. Then she went so far as to take his sight away from him by having hot iron rods used on him. He would no longer be able to view the land because of the actions of Delilah and her Philistine handlers. There are people who exist to do nothing but to stop those who have climbed their mountains from surveying the land. During the moments you hesitate to look upon the land, this is where you must decide upon your plan of action. Whitney Houston and her only child both fell victim to these types of predators. They both died tragically from falling into these traps.

When you look back over the lives of those two unfortunate women, you see that they lost themselves, their identities, and their reasons to be. The moment you find yourself spending more time on some else's problem, you need to step back and reassess that relationship. These people appear to be so needy. They can suck up all the oxygen in the room you share with them. They are selfish, and so demanding until you will work yourself to death trying to fix them. All the while you are dying. If you do die, they will be looking for the next victim to take your place.

Then there are the nemeses who plant the parasitic worm of self-doubt within your thoughts. Jesus ran upon this many times

during his earthly ministry. One case in particular was when the
five thousand who followed him out into the wilderness needed to
be fed. All but one of his disciples urged him to send them away.
They could not possibly see how all those people could be fed, when
there were no places to buy provisions. Only one of his disciples
went into action when Jesus commanded them to feed the masses.
He left and returned with a young lad. The lad had two little fish and
five small barley loaves of bread. With this Jesus fed the multitude,
and when everyone had eaten his or her fill, there were twelve full
baskets of food left. When you are confronted with doubters who
want to tell you what is impossible, you need to remember how you
got to where you are now. You climbed mountains that others would
not have dared to challenge. You faced freezing cold, slippery slopes,
and dangers seen and unseen. You kept moving towards the other
side of the mountains until you made it through them. You did not
come this far by challenging fate, only to be stopped by doubt. Doubt
is for cowards. Doubt is for the faint hearted. You may be tired from
your journey, but always remember destiny rewards the bold.

Look out for those who would place detours before you. Once
I overheard two women talking. One was telling the other about the
new man in her life. She said that she hoped he would marry her
because she needed help taking care of some things needing to be
attended to in her house. I waited to hear what else she had to say,
but the two of them changed the subject and began talking about the
new store opening in the strip mall. I pondered what I had heard. Not
once did I hear the woman say to the other woman that she loved the
man she was seeing. She was all about business, and matter-of-factly,
about her aims and ambitions. She really should have been telling
her girlfriend that what she really needed was a better paying job, or

she needed a raise at the one she already had. No, she was aiming at trapping the man she was seeing so he could improve her standard of living. I continue to say that men are romantic and women are sentimental. When a man loves a woman, he literally cannot keep his mind on anything else. The man loves the sound of his beloved's voice more than an unborn child loves his or her mother's voice inside the womb. He loves the scent of her presence and the little things like the way she laughs, or the way she looks into his eyes.

There are some women who marry for love, but there are too many who marryfor opportunities. This is historical in that women were married off to men to form alliances, to gain territory, but seldom were they permitted to marry for love. Some women still continue to marry for security. I remember hearing so many women saying, "I learned to love him." This is the selling of one's self for economic security and not the giving of one's self in love. There have always been users, but there were times when a woman and a man married for love. She wanted to have his babies and raise them together. He wanted to protect her and to provide for the family. He and she both wanted to grow old together. And during the winter period of their union, each wanted to be inseparable from the other. Unfortunately, today many women and men use the other person as a stepping stone, to acquire things and wealth. When the finance is gone, so is the romance. What happened to the vow, "until death do us part?"

The woman I overheard talking about marriage is a user. She is seeking to take the covenant of matrimony and turn it into an employment at will arrangement. She does not want a partnership with her man. What she wants is a joint venture with him. She wants a setup that allows her to stay married as long as she is getting more than she is giving. It is as if she is saying she will do what is expected of a wife as long as she gets what she wants. And if things change or are not to her liking, she will end the marriage. This is certainly an issue among Black men and Black women dating. I suspect it goes across color lines to affect relationships with other ethnic groups, too. What is disappointing here is one person uses another person for material things. Things come and go at the blinking of an eye. Love bears all, believes all, and endures all (I Corinthians 13). Love hides a multitude of faults and looks beyond one's faults and sees one's needs. Hopefully, if you are a man or a woman with means, you will not fall for a trap like the above. Let me end the discussion about resolve and doubters with the following.

Another way of looking at doubters is to read the book about Steve Jobs, the founder of Apple. There is also a new movie about him at the cinema, or you can get a DVD from Red Box and see it. Steve Jobs was a peculiar character; some would call him weird or strange. But you have to give him credit for what he accomplished in life. He took technology and gave the world the user-friendly Apple computer, the iPhone, the iPod, and iPad. He took an idea out of the family's garage and turned it into a truly global enterprise. Jobs climbed mountains to make Apple the number one software, computer, technology, and phone system in the world. He crossed huge mountains to get to where he was as the head and CEO of the company. But suddenly Steve looked around the board room and saw a room full of doubters. The stock prices were down and creativity seem to be stagnant. The board members voted to replace Steve, despite his protestations. They allowed their doubts about Steve to cast him aside. But unlike so many people, Steve did not lose faith in himself or in his abilities. He knew from climbing the mountains to get to the chair of the board that delays, troubles, and setbacks were to be expected. But most of those in the board room hadn't experienced what he himself had gone through. They voted him out of the chair, and removed him as the head of the company. In any other situation you or I might have doubted ourselves, but Steve had the singularity of his vision and extreme confidence in himself. Stop! You need to know that you cannot kill the dream in the dreamer. No one living can extinguish the fire burning deep within the mind of the visionary. And so it was with Steve Jobs.

The company began losing more and more market share, and the value of its stocks were at their lowest point. As bad as the one man who knew Steve the best and who still voted to remove him, he had to acknowledge that the company needed Steve. With shame and trepidation, they brought Steve back to rescue Apple. Steve, like Hannibal the Great, turned around the deep plunge into insolvency. The two titans took so little and did so much with it. Steve could see, as he looked out once before and now again, that the land was still opened up. He gave the technology of tomorrow to the everyday man and women of today. Steve turned Apple around. Nearly everywhere you look there is an Apple product. All of this is because Steve Jobs' vision was greater than the sum total of the common world's ability to see. He did not allow their doubts in him to get in the way of the visions that were jumping to get out of him. Real visionaries are not held down by misfortune. They've been through the mountains, and they know this is to be expected. Perhaps you are surrounded by doubters? If you are, never allow them to come between your views of the land.

I allowed this once, and spent precious years doubting my abilities to get my MBA degree. I allowed a kindergarten buddy to talk me out of striving to make this vision real. He criticized my poor undergraduate grades and how I just managed to obtain my bachelor's degree. I went twenty years thinking I was not smart enough to get this degree. Silly was I for allowing him to set my life's course, and its agenda. But after managing to graduate from divinity school and being able to pastor several congregations, I began to doubt the doubter. In 2001, still afraid, I went to my first class at Fontbonne University at St. Louis. I was supposed to be taking this task on with my niece. And wouldn't you know it, she dropped out of the program after the first night. I was highly upset and still somewhat afraid, but I refused to forfeit any of the hard borrowed tuition money.

I worked nights and studied before I went to classes in the evenings. I was determined to finish what I started. Let me tell you how determination and faith will make you stronger than you think you are. I managed to graduate on time. I did not know it, but as I was putting on my academic stole, cap, and gown, I was taken back to the time when I was about thirteen. I was on my bed resting. I was looking up thinking about what I wanted to be. And it was there that I saw myself as someone in business for himself. Our visions never die! We can push them aside and pretend they aren't there, but our visions are the land opened up before us. There will be people who will attempt to keep you from claiming what the land has to offer you. In moments of stress and conflict, remember what you did to get here. Call upon the inner strength of your total being to give you the will to go around your barriers. What you will be facing are not mountains, they are just speed bumps in the middle of the road you have chosen to travel.

I suspect some of you have made it through the mountains not knowing you were given divine help along the way. You could just be climbing down the mountains, and you are looking at the broad expansive of the land. You are clueless as to what this phase of your life's journey will bring. Can you decide to use your talents and exceptionalism to stop global warming and climate change? Have you considered finding a way to stop overfishing the oceans of the world? Will you work to bring a permanent end to the senseless wars in the Middle East? Can you help America find its way again? I am certain you can solve these problems and all the others that have taken humanity and life as we know it to the cliff of our demise. All you need to do is to listen to your dreams, your visions, and the still small voice speaking to your souls. One final thought. You can do, become, and make anything you set your minds to do.

Readers Notes

The Only Free Lunches
Came from Jesus

LET US JUST PRESUPPOSE YOU HAVE MADE IT THROUGH THE MOUNTAINS and you have accumulated an appreciable amount of wealth. As you come into the land you will find many standing before you with quick schemes to make you even wealthier. If you have recently retired or are about to retire, you have been flooded by invitations to dinners where you can investigate investing for your retirement years. An immediate red flag should be the offer of a free lunch (in this case a dinner). There is nothing free in life except trouble; it comes with the territory. All of these investment companies do more taking of your hard-earned savings than they do any adding to them. Drive down any street in your city or town and there are investment firms after investment firms. These people are building and opening new offices with your money. You are financing their steady growth. The stock market is not paying off for the common man or woman. You lose going into the deal and when you exit the deal. This is because the investment firms use arbitrage formulas to make high-speed computer transitions. Nearly every time you want to make a trade, you have done it too late to make a profit. Then there are the hedge funds that are set up to burn the unsuspecting suckers. Your best strategy to make money is to invest it in insurance companies. They pay a percentage point or two above what the banks are offering, and they have a guaranteed return. Whatever you do, please do not allow flattery and greed to fleece you wallets. You have gone through too much to give your earnings away.

Football players, actors, and musicians often make the mistake of overspending. I recently saw the rapper and actor known as Fifty Cent in *The New York Times*. He was dressed to the nines, and over in another section of the newspaper was an article about him filing for bankruptcy. He is just one of many celebrities who burn through fortunes before they realize what they have done. The majority of the R & B artists sold millions of dollars in records. But when they were no longer in demand, they had little or nothing to show for their work. I have a rule for you that will ensure your future. Invest 10 to 25 percent of what you make. This can be in housing developments, insurance savings, or your own IRS accounts. If you do this you will have something to rely on when times get rough.

Also, don't forget to keep the people who were with you when you were going through the mountains. They helped you and you them to make it through hard and difficult times. They had your back, and in most cases, they will continue to do so. Nevertheless, always do what Ronald Reagan said, "Trust but verify." You may have come down from the mountain with your wits about you, but others may not have. Should this be the case, you may be able to persuade them to follow your plan of thought. Together you can form a team to keep you all from falling prey to flattery and disingenuous proposals.

One can go on and on about what lies before you when you make it through the mountains. What a person does when he or she looks out onto the land is important. The journey is not over.

Once you or anyone else makes it through the mountains, you must continue journeying through life and situations you confront. Life is always a struggle for purpose and meaning. Meaning is most often found in the journey and not at the end of the destination. So wherever you are now, stop, take time to view your surroundings. And once you have assessed the lay of the land, go into it with wisdom, experience, and confidence. And finally always remember: Once you get through the mountains, the land opens up.

 *Readers Notes*

The Road You are On is the One You Should be On

TIME AND TIME AGAIN, I have heard people say "If I would have only done …" Looking back at one's choices takes away the ability to focus on opportunities that lie ahead. It is extremely difficult to walk forward all the while you are looking back. People who attempt to do this trip over something and they fall on their backsides. To those who have made it through the mountains, there is no time to second guess their actions. If they even entertain the notion of returning to the places where they first began their journeys, they are foolish at best. There is an old saying that says, "There is no sense in going over already plowed ground." Besides, there is a strong probability that they wouldn't be able to make it back, knowing the challenges of their journeys. These people are in between visions. Their top visions were getting through the mountains. Now, since they have made it through to the other side, they are at a loss.

A case in point, I was talking with a fellow recently. It was apparent he had made it through his mountains. Despite some major health issues he was in a far better position to recover, and if not recover, to manage his condition. He was making a six-figure income. He had an adoring and considerate wife, and he had stepchildren who dearly loved him. Yet he talked about what life for him would have been if he had remained in Iowa. He had a "fair-to-middling" job when he was in Iowa. The job paid a living wage, and it wasn't as difficult as the work he found when he moved to Texas. But what he didn't understand was that he, like so many Texans, came there with little or nothing and reinvented themselves. He and the other Texans were better off financially and physically than those who re-mained behind. As he talked, I got him to speak of all the places he had traveled to since moving to Texas. He recited places in Europe, Asia, South America, cities throughout the United States, and then he shared his upcoming cruise to Jamaica. All of a sudden he real-ized that despite his health issues, his life wasn't bad at all. When he looked at the divorce that took place soon after moving to Texas, he saw that the first wife was moving out of the way for him to get with the loving one he now has. And when he talked about not having children of his own, I stopped him. I reminded him of the fact that the children that came with his wife love him dearly. I spelled out to him why they loved him so. I explained to him that they see how his marrying their mother gave them a role model of what a real father is. And his love was unconditional to them. He bought them the things they needed, and he did for them just because. Suddenly he began to see how blessed, lucky, and fortunate he was. The road he took was and still is the road he was supposed to take.

This friend and many like him fail to see and to understand the many roads one can travel to claim his or her destiny. The mountains that we made it through opened up new possibilities. But somehow, they thought their journeys where the end-all. If you have made it through your mountains, accept the fact that the view is entirely different from the one you saw on the other side of the mountains, and while going through the mountains. Accepting this fact, they need to clear their thoughts. Their minds must not equate where they now stand with where they once stood. Coming through the mountains presents each traveler with his or her own unique view. No matter what has opened up before them, there are opportunities to be had. They have to remove fear of the unknown from their thoughts. Where they now stand is far less dangerous than where they came from, and what they went through to get to those points.

You have seen what I am expressing. There have been celebrities who have made it big, then unexpectedlythey flame out. They dove into drug addiction. They then began living pathological lies. They appear to be exhibiting survivor's remorse. One should not feel guilty because he or she made it, and others did not. If you feel too blessed or fortunate, you can share your skills, treasure, and time. To placate this feeling, one can reach back and assist others who are on their journeys through the mountains. What they can also do, when feelings of unworthiness or inadequacies assault their psyches, is to look at what they sacrificed to make it through the mountains. Doing this they will remember what perils and dangers they endured to be where they stand. This was done with the aid of God, fortune, and dogged determination. Never allow shame to paralyze you. Look around you and see if there is someone who has just made it through the mountains. When you find him or her, be a ready guide, sage, and friend to that person. But never ever come between that individual and his or her personal destiny.

Personally I look back, and I get religious. I think of the old gospel song entitled, "How I Got Over." Growing up as a child, I didn't live on the other side of the tracks. My family and I lived surrounded by the tracks. On every side of the little parcel of ground on which the public housing we called home rested, there were railroad tracks. I can't for the life of me understand how eight and sometimes ten people managed to live in a tiny three-bedroom apartment. There is no way in hell that I want to go back to those days. Living in the "projects" was not the good ol' days. In fact, living there inspired me and most of my family to climb the mountains, and to go to college to obtain viable educations. Looking back over from whence I came is humbling. I know where I've been. As I look at the land, I don't know where I am going. But I know that as long as I have my health and strength, there are possibilities before me. When I get unsettled in my thoughts, I look at where I now reside. I give thanks to God for the place where I now live.

As a little boy, when I crossed the tracks to go to the business sections of the two towns on the other side, I would look and hope. I saw what to me were mansions. There were ranch homes, with yards where the grass grew. Sidewalks and curbs were free of trash. I could only wish and hope to someday own one of those houses. I was determined to graduate from high school and then to go through college with a diploma. I managed to do this, and when I did, my vision changed. You see, college was my journey that took me to the other side. While there, the land opened up before me. My perspective radically changed. The houses outside of the projects were now seen as starter homes. And the people living in them were just those who managed to live on the other side of the tracks. It was like they were keeping us hemmed in, while they were stuck where they were.

I now live in a new subdivision in Edwardsville, Illinois. When the wife and I decided to move from her "Sears Cape Cod" house to one we both own, there was some friction. She instinctively wanted to look at homes in our subdivision that were previously owned. While I insisted we only look at newly built homes. She asked me why I was so adamant in getting a home without a previous owner. I shared with her that in the homes with previous owners, we were buying their dreams. We were purchasing things they wanted and valued. But with a brand new home, we could impart our dreams and wishes. I share this because sometimes when we look at the land before us, we look at the open expanses through the eyes, dreams, and realities of those who came before us. It is all right to look at what those who came before us have done. However, it is not all right to make what they saw and did our journey's end. This is really just another way of looking back at what you left and feeling it is better than the possibilities that lay ahead. I am convinced the land on the other side of the mountains is open to new ideas, new opportunities, new wealth, new lives, and new discoveries.

Something else about what my friend was sharing has come to mind. Deep within him was the wound of his failed marriage. He somehow looked at moving to Texas as the cause of the breakup. In my line of sight, his former wife had emotionally moved on from their relationship. She moved to be with someone who was running from her. She did not understand this until years after they divorced. By then she was alone, and my friend was with his new wife and family. In a way she was looking backwards all the while she was moving herself and my friend to Texas. One can only speculate on what could have been for the two of them if only they had stayed together and looked at the land that opened up before them. In her case, she was the loser. She did not get the man she broke her home up for, and she lost the man who loved her without reservation. She allowed what could have been to be high jacked by an outside interloper. The lesson I get from this is that when you get through the mountains, look at what lies before you. My friend has not allowed the wound of his failed marriage to heal. Hopefully with deep thought and understanding he will see the flowers in the garden he has made for himself.

I have come to recognize in my senior years of life that everyone and everything is replaceable. My friend replaced the husband who left his current wife and children. His new wife replaced the former wife who left him for a fellow who did not want her. And all of this is to impress upon the minds of those going through divorces what is written above. After you climb through your mountains of utter sadness and come out on the other side, you will have a new look on life. Those who have recently lost a spouse or a loved one and have gone through the mountains and come through to the other side-will be looking at lands that open their lives up to new hopes, joys, and fulfillments. Just keep on walking. Do not content yourselves to remain in that moment. On the other side of grief are new joy, new love, and new healing.

Readers Notes

Coming Down and Making your Own Tracks

IF YOU LOOK THROUGH THE EYES OF YOUR IMAGINATIONS, you see many footprints leading off into the distance. Here is where many make critical mistakes. Many choose to walk in the footprints left behind by others. It is vitally important that you do not do this! You are where you are because you left the confining demands and rules of the others behind to make it to this point in your lives. You drowned out their opinions as to what it was you had to do. You refused to conform. Now, on this side of the mountains, don't re-enslave yourselves to convention and choose to walk in someone else's footprints. You did not get through the mountains to be like everyone else. The footprints before you were left by individuals who went off in different directions to follow their own individual destinies. Try as you will, you cannot duplicate someone else's success and claim it as yours. No, it is obligatory of you to step where others have not stepped. You made it through the mountains to become different. Walking in your own path will see to you becoming inimitably different from those who came before you and those who will follow after you.

Although there are millions of footprints leading to the open land, there are places where no man or woman has yet stepped. Looking back at history, only the person who has done something first is given the greater credit. Those who improved upon their discoveries and inventions are given honorable mentions, but they will never be remembered as the ones who were first. Alexander Graham Bell will forever be remembered as the inventor of the telephone. Thomas Edison, the inventor of the first practical light bulb, is the person we think of when we turn on our lights. George Washington Carver made countless inventions from the lowly peanut, sweet potato, soybean, and pecans. Dr. Daniel Hale Williams was the first surgeon to successfully perform open-heart surgery. Dr. Ernest Everett Just became a noted authority on marine biology with his publishing of over fifty papers on the subject. And there is Dr. Aprille Ericsson, the noted mechanical engineer who proposed bringing dust back from the surface of Mars to be examined. I could go on and on, but you get the point. Every one of these individuals did their own thing. The land on this side of the mountain has opened up incredible opportunities for you.

The problem with most of America is the lack of adventurous creativity, audacity, and daring. The majority of Americans want to work for somebody. They want someone to hire them so they can work forty hours a week to get a paycheck. This is part of the problem with the economy today. The forefathers and foremothers struck out north, south, and west to discover, grow, and to build new things and businesses. They were men and women of enterprise, initiative, innovation, boldness, and get-up-and-go. You are on the other side of the mountains because deep within your DNA is the stuff of which our forebears were made. The old saying, "Opportunity goes to the prepared," continues to apply here where you are standing. There truly is no excuse for the way many people live today in America. There are millions of men, women and children living below the poverty level. Most of them are there because they succumbed or acceded to the voices of those around them. Those voices have imprisoned them to live on the narrow shores of scarcity and insufficient resources. Remember, this is where you were prior to your journey through the mountains. Going through the mountains was dangerous, but walking in someone else's footsteps places you in danger of re-enslavement on this side of the mountains. Strange as it seems, life is not a destination. Life is a series of trips, adventures, ventures, and journeys you take throughout your entire existence. People who are doing things and making new products and inventions are too busy on their journeys to carry you all the way with them. It is incumbent of you to make your own trails in life as you go into the open land before you.

The only thing stopping you is you. You must take the first steps on fresh open ground. You must call upon that spirit that drove, compelled, and obligated you to climb the mountains to get through to the other side. The greatest sin you can commit now is settling for another's destiny. You and I have run across individuals who married and placated, propitiated their own dreams and desires for the other spouse. They were the other spouse's biggest cheerleader. Suddenly, the other spouse delivered the boom and asked for a divorce. The relationship began as a codependent one, but now the other spouse is independent. He or she is an individual (not divided), and you are no longer needed, wanted, or tolerated. This is the same for the worker who wants to work for someone else instead of for himself or herself. You add value and wealth to their portfolio while adding little or nothing to your own. With technology being as prolific as it is, the old Marxist adage of "supply and demand ..." does not mean as much. Labor does not depend on as many hands to produce a product. An entrepreneur at home with a computer is capable of producing millions of dollars of intellectual property which he or she can sell for profit. More billions of dollars are being made using the Internet than are being made by all the working steel mills throughout the world. You are obligated to make your own pathways in life and not follow in the footsteps of others.

Look at Bill and Hillary Clinton for an example. Bill was always the front person in their marriage. He was the governor of Arkansas, and she was the First Lady. It was the scandal of Bill while he was in the White House that compelled or nudged Hillary Clinton to walk on her own pathway. She did not physically leave the marriage. She remained Mrs. Bill Clinton, the First Lady. However, when Bill's term ended, Hillary struck out on her own journey. She moved to New York State and ran to become one of that state's United States senators. She won one term, and she won a second term. Hillary later ran to become president of the United States, but she lost the Democratic nomination to Senator Barack Obama. This was a painful loss for Hillary, but grace reached out to her and she became a member of President Obama's Cabinet. She served as the secretary of state until she resigned to run a second time for the presidency. People who knew them both always said Hillary was as smart, if not smarter, than Bill. Hillary Clinton has an impressive resume.

All this being said and noted, ask if this is what she truly wanted in life? Was becoming the first female president of the United States of America her burning desire, or was it Bill's? Going into the election the polls showed her to be the runaway favorite. However, when the election results were totaled, she lost badly in the Electoral College votes. The people voted for Donald Trump in the firewall states, and they gave him the victory. The press and talking heads have come up with many reasons as to why Hillary lost the election. They attribute her defeat to everything from her personal server, the foundation she and Bill established, her Wall Street speaking fees, her being a woman, and the emails found on Anthony Weiner's computer during the last week of the election. These were all symptoms of the true reason why Hillary lost the election. I strongly believe she lost the election because she was running for Bill Clinton and others who wanted her to run.

When a person lives the dream of another, he or she ultimately fails. The person fails because he or she lacks the drive and the burning will to live their purpose and destiny. The mountains you came through may be similar to Hillary's mountain. There could be a plethora of things or events that started you on your journeys, but you made it through. Now don't let the dreams of others supersede your dreams. Always remember, you did not leave the crowd on the other side of the mountains only to join in with another crowd on this side of the mountain. This would be a sin and a shame if you looked at all the land opened up to you, only to look down and begin your walk in the footprints left by others. The funny thing is, people have an instinctive sense of a person's authenticity. I felt deep within me that Bernie Sanders was the better candidate on the Democratic side. I so wanted him to run and be the alternative vision of change. Trump's message of change seemed to be one of retrenchment of European racism and top-down economics. His vision appeared to me to be that of taking the nation back to the days when environmental problems were ignored and minorities were tolerated. As it is, Donald

Trump is the elected president of the United States. Trump came across as authentic to the majority of people who were fed up with the inequities that have gone on for more than twenty years. I only hope and pray he will not move too far to the right of center. And I hope both parties in Congress will come together to work together to defend and to protect the Constitution of the United States. As a loyal citizen, I pray for the newly elected president. I want him to make all of America great again. Now let's reflect back on what a person needs to do when they make it through the mountains. Let's examine the correct way to enter the land.

 *Readers Notes*

Walk with Your Head on a Swivel

YOU GET YOURSELF TOGETHER ENOUGH TO BEGIN WALKING the vast expanses of the land. The first and most important thing you need to always remember is to constantly scan your environment. There are great opportunities where you are headed, and there are dangers and possibilities of great loss. You will have to keep your guard up 24/7. Believe it or not there will be people who will help you along the way and others who will take advantage of you if you are naïve and foolish. The world of business has a simple exercise one can do. It is known as "SWOT." SWOT forces you to look for things that will strengthen your economic, spiritual, and physical self. And it will force you to look for things that will weaken you in those areas. Always be on the lookout for opportunities that can advance you spiritually, economically, and socially, and threats that can harm you. Know your present weaknesses and future ones that can and will evolve throughout your life's journeys. Always remember your journeys are not fair promenades. Your journeys will determine the quality of life you will live. Your journeys will determine the homes you will live in and the influence you will project in the various communities you will become affiliated with over time.

Most of us are aware of our strengths. We know the physical

limitations of our bodies. We know the things we are inherently just good at doing. These things are blessings and curses that can lift you up or they can tear you down. All throughout history great men and women have risen and fallen because their strengths also became their weaknesses. The majority of these men and women were imbued with natural charisma. They drew men and women to their sides to take up their causes and make them their own. They oozed a pheromone that caused their followers to give of themselves freely and without reservation. The men and women who have such strengths and powers use them again and again to rally the masses. What they forget is the strength of their charisma becomes weaker and weaker with each application. It is like crack cocaine. The first time one tries it there is an unbelievable high and a feeling of euphoria. But after this passes, each time the drug is inhaled the highs become less intense and the feelings of euphoria become shorter and shorter. Some addicts find themselves behaving like dogs chasing their tails. And over time they come to see the objects of their adoration as their personal weakness. They turn on them or abandon them with little or no advance warnings. And the people who were fanatics become mobs of vengeance. If you are on the receiving end of the mob, your fate will be similar to Libya's Moammar Gadhafi. He ruled for forty-two years, but when his reign ended, it was a bloody one for him. It is apparent by now that your strength can also be your weakness. Samson of the Hebrew Scriptures was just such a person whose strength—if not his weakness—caused him to falter.

The story of Samson and Delilah is one everybody has heard at church, in the temple, or at the mosque. As the story goes, Samson had incredible strength. He killed a lion with just his hands, and he killed many Philistines with the jaw bone of an ass. He was a hero of Israel, but he liked the women of his enemy more than he cared to defend his people. The Philistines were undone by Samson; he could not be contained by them. Time after time when they surrounded him they came out on the short end of the stick. They tried everything they could to bind him, but nothing would hold him. It took the cunning of a Philistine woman named Delilah to subdue him. She used her sexuality to get to his ego. Once she was there, she used cunning seduction to find the source of his strength. On more than one occasion, Delilah thought she had obtained the answer to what was needed to subdue and bind Samson. Each time Samson told her a lie. When the Philistines came to bind Samson, he made short work of them. But persistence paid off for Delilah and staying too long with a known enemy was Samson's downfall. Perhaps in a moment of high passion, Samson told her what she wanted to know about him. Whatever the cause, he confided to her that his strength was in his hair. If you don't know anything about Samson, allow me to fill you in now. He was an anointed person, "set aside" as a savior of his people. The sign of his uniqueness was his long, uncut hair. As long as he did not cut his hair, he had the strength to prevail against his people's enemy, the Philistines. Finding the true source of Samson's strength, Delilah shared this information with the Philistines. And she was rewarded with much gold. Her sexual favors weakened his ability to live up to his purpose and calling in life. Her favors loosened his tongue and clouded his ability to think about what telling an alien and an enemy of his people would do to them and to him in the long run. Finding the man's weakness, while he slept Delilah took shears in hand and cut off Samson's locks. When the deed was completed, she called in the enemy, the Philistine soldiers, and they subdued Samson. Weakened and now defenseless, Samson was bound. The

Philistines soldiers took hot irons and pressed them into Samson's eyes, blinding him. Samson failed to truly live up to his destiny in life. At the end of the story, we read of the last act of redemption he is given. Blinded and in chains, Samson calls upon the Lord to allow him to die along with his enemies. Granting him this prayer, Samson was given a full measure of his strength. With this gift, he pushes down the load-bearing pillars of the Philistine temple. With this deed he and the Philistines perished in the rubble.

You can go to the Bible and read the rest of the story. What I want to impress upon you is that your strength is probably also your weakness. Too much pride can become your weakness—just as too little courage can stand between you and conquest. Moderation is the vehicle one needs to ride on into the open land. Macy's Department Stores is a good case in point of what I am trying to get across. The company will close one hundred of its less profitable stores so it can compete against Amazon, Kohl's, and Walmart. As with any ongoing concern, Macy's saw itself as the premiere department store. What it failed to understand was that it must constantly be watching for internal and external threats. In life, the failure to adapt to the changes in your environment means certain death. Doing things the way you have always done things goes beyond tradition. It slides you closer and closer to obsolescence and extinction. In the vastness of the land you must constantly be about change. You must change the way you look at things, people, situations, ways of doing things, and what you need to do to remain viable for yourself and to others.

Today the top retailer—online and outright—is Amazon. Moving to try and topple Amazon is Walmart. Walmart wants to regain its status as the number one retailer. Amazon is a threat to Walmart because it has cut into its profits along with its market shares and those of Macy's, Kohl's, J.C. Penney, and Nordstrom. Walmart is an example of a company scanning to see what threats are on the horizon. It has deep financial pockets and seeing the increasing, steady growth of Amazon it is moving aggressively into the online sales section. The company just paid $3.3 billion dollars for the e-commerce startup Jet.com. What remains to be seen is can it catch up with Amazon's sales? What it appears Walmart is doing is noting Amazon as a threat. And seeing this as such, Walmart has accessed this to be a weakness in its corporate structure. Therefore, Walmart is moving to confront Amazon on its own playing field. Walmart has its corporate head on a swivel. It scans the horizon constantly to determine its strengths, its weaknesses, its opportunities, and its threats. Perhaps it waited too long before confronting Amazon. Nevertheless, the real "canary in the mine" could be none other than the small grocery chain known as Aldi.

Aldi drove Walmart out of Germany in 2006, and forced it to abandon Germany's lucrative $370 billion retail grocery market. There are many possible reasons why this David of a chain defeated Walmart, the giant Goliath. What is factual is this small grocery chain soundly and conveniently defeated the mighty Walmart. Like being stung by a bee, Walmart has imprinted upon its corporate memory this defeat. Now as Aldi expands here in the United States, Walmart is setting up "firewalls" to contain Aldi from cutting deeper into its grocery shares. A case in point, Walmart has the lowest prices for a dozen of eggs on sales in its stores. This is a loss leader for the corporation. This is done to increase the traffic of grocery shopping at its stores instead of at Aldi. The giant views Aldi as a growing threat, and it is moving to contain it now. However, Aldi continues to grow by opening new stores in transitioning neighborhoods that have been, and are being, abandoned by the "big box stores." Aldi views these new stores as forts for growth and as gains in market share in the grocery market place. I must reveal that when I shop weekly for groceries, I instinctively go to my local Aldi store. I do this even though there is a Walmart Super Store just across the street from my Aldi's store. I go there because the price points are generally lower than Walmart's points are. I can stock up on things I use weekly and be out of the place within ten minutes or less. Last, I don't have to go to a self-checkout. Now when you go to Walmart you are forced to either stand in line at a checkout lane, or you go to the self-checkout area. Aldi seems to move the people out of its stores using real humans. Why can't Walmart do the same thing? I believe customer service is a key factor in Aldi's steady growth. Walmart sees Aldi as its up-and-coming threat, and Aldi seems to be positioning itself to take a lion's-size bite out of the largest grocery chain in America. Marketing strategy seems to be Aldi's strength and the opportunity other grocery chains failed to capitalize upon.

As for you, looking at these examples may better prepare you when you encounter the people and situations as you travel through the open land. Looking back at the scenarios presented, you can see that Aldi is not trying to "out Walmart" the grocery giant. It is using its own "out-in-the-fringes" strategy to expand its market share throughout the country. And it is doing it steadily and successfully. My son-in-law who is from Los Angeles came back to the Midwest last year and gleefully informed me that there is now an Aldi store there. Notice that he said there was only one when he shared this with me in 2015. What Aldi does is create demand by limiting its availability initially. Rarely does it advertise (most of this is done during the major holidays) because it uses word of mouth to stir the public's inquisitiveness.

This is sort of like what Donald Trump did and continues to do. President Trump comes out with over-the-top tweets. He then gets the news media to give him hours and hours of free air time. While they are spending time on what his tweets said or did not say, Trump has slipped in an executive order or a change in the way government has been run. He is a master at getting free PR, too. What might turn out to be a big problem is his mastery at creating so much confusion that you can't tell where he is leading the nation. This has the potential of causing grave problems on the international stage.

 *Readers Notes*

Do Not Allow Others to Dissuade You from Your Vision

IT HAS SUDDENLY DAWNED UPON ME that I neglected to remind you not to allow anyone here on the open land to dissuade you. You see, there are people in the open land who will use you, given the opportunity. There are, additionally, people who will try everything in the book to discourage you. You wouldn't have thought this to be a fact, but it is a reality. These people are similar to the ones you grew up with on the other side of the mountains. There were some whom you may have come into contact with while you were going through the mountains. But these are more cunning in their craft of discouragement.

They often appear to be encouraging and very interested in helping you to find your goal, or to become what your spirit guide or vision has called you to be. Nevertheless, if you drop your guard, they will cloud your vision and your intentions. They do this until you abandon your quest and direct your efforts to their all-consuming ones. They literally flip the switch on you. Now you are in a co-dependent situation where your life energy is being drained from your mind, body, and soul. This happens when you forget how those on the other side of the mountains tried their best to keep you from thinking about what lay on the other side. But you blocked out what they were saying, left them behind, and made it through to the open land. You were so resolute in accomplishing your vision, dream, quest, and destiny that when you were in the mountains, you would not remain there. There were people living pretty well in the mountains, but the inner voice calling to you compelled you to leave. And in leaving you came this far on your quest of discovery. So why are you listening to outside voices more intently than to the voice calling to you inwardly? Did not the inner voice, vision, or dream bring you safely and securely to where you are now? If this is true, then awake from your non-restive slumber and reclaim your life.

These interlopers are not your friends, and they mean you more harm than good. They begin your association with them as helpful friend. As time progresses, they monopolize almost all of your time and energy, and they separate you from your journey in the open land. Soon you listen more to them than you do to your own mind and common sense. They can get you so confused that you will see reality through their filters and not as it naturally appears. You have been misappropriated at this point on your journey. You don't even know if you love the person or if you hate him or her. Just as an addict, you are emotionally addicted to them. And we all know how addicts eventually die castoff lives by their sources of addiction. Whatever you do, when you get to the open land do not value the other person's opinions of you and about you, more than you value yourself. These people are like crabs. They are in dark places, and they cannot get out. And when they see you crawling out of the dark basket, they reach up and grab hold of you and begin pulling you down where they are. Always guard your thoughts. Keep your vision always in sight. Never allow another to edit it, change it, or alter it. What God has given to you is for you exclusively. You vision, dream, goal, or calling is yours and yours alone. Do not relinquish it for carnal pleasures of the flesh or for flattery. Learn to judge a person not by what he or she says, but by what he or she does. If you don't learn how to do this, they will soon have you wrapped up like a moth in a spider's web.

From time to time you need to meditate on what the Lord has told you to do, or to be, in life. See how close you are to being there. Ask yourself if the other person is demanding more of you than he or she is giving back to you. If you are consistently on the short end of the stick, then you need to terminate that relationship posthaste because in the open land you have a finite amount of time to get to where you are supposed to be going. You have only so much energy to take you there and you cannot get there carrying dead weight. Making it plain, any relationship that denies you from seeking your vision is not the one you need to pursue.

I know of a beautiful young woman who has lost herself in the open land. She is in a cruel and destructive relationship with a wraith or life-force sucker. This poor child is like so many young women and men. They reach out and grab the lower hanging fruit on the tree of opportunity. These pieces of fruit are often damaged and bruised. They are easy to come by, but they aren't the ones a person should desire. This young woman is in a seesaw relationship with a "crack" dealer. She has spent, begged, and borrowed her future income and savings to get him out of jail. Instead of being grateful to her, he beats her, steals from her, and has taken her with him on the long, dark descent into addiction. Her mother, father, and family have tried to get her back on the right road, but nothing can persuade her to leave hell for open land. She will most likely come to her senses when she is hollowed out by mental, physical, and drug abuse. Most likely by then she will have used up her most precious resource of time along with her treasure. The spider offers the moth any and everything to entice it to leave the route it set out to travel. And when the moth alights upon the web, it is trapped and becomes a tasty morsel for the spider. My advice is not to allow the outside voices to drown out the small, still voice calling deep from within you. Please take a moment or two and think about what was just presented. Then go on and consider the part that comes after this.

 *Readers Notes*

Don't Jump In at the Middle of a Surge

THERE IS A FIFTY-YEAR-OLD WOMAN I KNOW who wants to become an entrepreneur. Don't become sexist or ageist, either, as I relate the rest of the story to you. You are never too old to follow your dream or vision. Julia Child was an older woman when she became an international cooking sensation. And we now know about Florence Foster Jenkins who took her vision of singing at Carnegie Hall and turned it into reality. She was an older woman with limited singing abilities. She took a pathway that others thought was impracticable and foolish, but for her it was the right road to travel. As for the woman I know who wants to become an entrepreneur, the good part about her is that she has a dream, a vision. She also has women like the ones I just mentioned to follow for inspiration. The women cited and the woman we are talking about, had and have the advantage over you. Most of you have come all this way and you don't know what the hell you are doing here. You cannot for the life of you see yourselves moving out and into the open land before you. This woman is different, and she knows there is something for her out there in the new land. What she has to guard against is stepping into the footprints of others and being taken advantage of by them.

So should she follow her dream? Should you follow your

dream? Yes, to both of the questions. What you and she might consider doing is looking for untapped markets. Yes, in her case, go for the low-hanging fruit instead of trying to climb the trees to get at the fruit hanging at the top. What if she looked at all the people eating takeout? What if this woman set up a business model that allowed people in her city to order take out from their preferred vendors and her business delivers the take outs, on time and in good condition, with a nominal surcharge tacked on to the delivery cost? With a computer, fax machine, and cell phone she can receive and process the orders timely. She would then need a logistics network to get the meals to the clients. Now this can be done by using Uber drivers who are waiting for clients, or the local taxi companies in her city. In cities where there are bicycle messengers and delivery riders, they can be freelance employees. Using this model this woman can become the entrepreneur she dreams of becoming. Age is no longer a limiter of one's ambitions, but time continues to be a factor. Remember, Julia Child wasn't a spring chicken when she became a cooking sensation. And Col. Sanders was white-haired when he made Kentucky Fried Chicken a part of millions of Americans' Sunday dinner meals.

What I want you and others to understand is the need to go for the inventions, products, and services that no one else has developed or have they offered. The new watch word of this century is innovation and not the rebranding of old things. For examples of rebranding, McDonald's and Panera Bread Company are advertising that their foods will become all-natural, free of chemical steroids, preservatives, and artificial colorings—"all good stuff." It is nice to know that the fast-food industry and other suppliers of packaged foods are moving in this direction. But will this increase the growth of their industries? Perhaps, but I tend to think it will not because these companies are only moving in this direction because of the FDA. The FDA is requiring them to remove many additives now in their foods. Many of them are not needed, and they are suspected to be possible causes of obesity. These steps taken by restaurants and fast-food chains to serve foods absent of hormones, artificial coloring, and taste enhancers, are welcomed and needed, however, most likely this will be nominal growth for them. Absent of these additives Americans could lose some weight, and this is beneficial to all of us who eat out.

In case you haven't noticed it, we Americans are some fat people. Include myself in this observation. Drive or walk down any city or town and one will see people who are not just fat, they are obese! Why is this so? Might the eating of prepackaged, over-processed food be the culprit? Or is it because Americans are not as physically active as they once were, and still they continue to eat the way they have always eaten? I suspect both of these questions are reasons why we Americans are so fat. I know I am fat. I am twenty to twenty-five pounds overweight. And outside of me walking about fifteen miles a week and lifting weights when I can, I yo-yo between losing and gaining ten pounds. At least I am trying, but what about the people in America's inner cities? They do not have the large grocery stores down the street where they can purchase fresh meats, fish, fruits, and vegetables. They mostly have access to the stores run by the newly arrived immigrants who stock fast and prepackaged foods. They also spend more for these unhealthy foods than one would ordinarily purchase at a grocery store chain. This is not happening, because these people are America's 47 percenters (the percentage of Americans who pay no income tax, according to remarks by former presidential candidate Mitt Romney). They are the underclass poor living in the abandoned inner cities and those who live in the hidden poverty of rural America. They either eat too much of the wrong foods or they go to bed hungry, and both are malnourished. These group settings are areas where the entrepreneur can make his or her mark and render a service to the needy.

As helpful as the federal and state food programs have been, people continue to fall through the cracks. This is due to a plethora of reasons that I will not go into here, but there are children in our cities and in our rural areas who would not get enough to eat if it wasn't for the school breakfast and lunch programs and for the after-school programs, as well. What you who are striking out on your own pathway can do is to develop model programs that can be successfully applied and marketed across the country. Abandoned factories and warehouses could be converted into urban greenhouses that produce fruits and vegetables which could then be sold locally to the undernourished and to local restaurants. These restaurants can be chains, or they could be niche market places where ethnic foods can be served. Either case, the food coming out of their kitchens will be garden fresh and free of chemicals. Think of the diversity in what Americans would be able to eat and the healthy benefits this idea offers, in comparison to what people are now eating.

Then there are the rural poor. They could use the acre or two that their trailer homes sit on to become part of cooperatives that sell to the large food chains and to the emerging markets in China, India, Africa, and the Middle East. These countries and regions have many of their populations living on less than the minimum daily food requirements. These are nations with billions of people who cannot feed their growing populations. America still has some of the world's richest farm land, the folk just need to put the land to good use. You or someone like you could make your way to where your destinies take you and still provide a service to the 47 percenters and the rest of the world. With this model, or one similar to it, you are walking where others haven't dared to walk. The possibilities are unlimited for you to network with others like yourself. The logistics could be solved by hiring the unemployed and unskilled workers to grow, prepare, package, and deliver the finished products. This is doable, and it is a market that hasn't really been addressed by the private sector.

Take a drive by any street in the inner city and you will find abandoned churches that go begging for someone to tear them down and build new affordable housing. They have other uses, too. These old churches could be turned into dance studios, restaurants, adult daycares, and apartments. Here is real estate that is cheap. Most of the mainline Christian denominations would gladly unload them. With these bargains, you or a partnership could segue with the local community college and trade unions to train and hire the chronic unemployed to rebuild their neighborhoods brick by brick. This is what is needed in urban settings. Black Americans cannot wait for the federal and state governments to solve their problems. This is something you and concerned visionaries like you can do for them, and for yourselves. You will be creating wealth and growth where others see only blight.

I have often driven along the highways and looked at the most beautiful and picturesque landscape and scenery in the world. America truly has some of the most breathtaking sights in the world. Why not go into these places with eyes of opportunities wide open? These rural towns and places are tourist spots to be developed. Seriously, they have just as much to offer as taking a cruise to the islands in the Caribbean or to Latin America. I have been there three times already and will go there again soon. What I discovered is that most of the ports of call don't offer me much different from what I see here in the States. I am just about exhausted from looking at towns, cities, and into the faces of poor people trying to sell me things that will not get through customs. Within forty miles of most cities are rural areas and little towns that have quaint and unique heritages. What underdeveloped opportunities await the people who can turn these into field trips for school children. They could be just the place for a family getaway. They are away, but still close to home.

I am thinking now of a little town close to where I live. The town is Grafton, Illinois. Grafton is the home of Illinois' Pere Marquette State Park, which is its largest state park. Where the park and town are located, the Illinois, the Missouri, and the Mississippi rivers converge or come together. The park had been the major draw of the city for years. The lodge there offers great food and a great place to commune with nature. There is good fishing in the slips that one can get to by boat or by taking the ferry to a small island known as Brussels. Now these things have been there for years. It took the flood of 1993 to cause someone in the town to have their "Eureka" moment. The flood covered the city up to the tall, steep bluffs. When it was over, many people built their new homes up above the river along the bluffs. Then suddenly there was a revitalization of the old buildings along the scenic highway leading into Grafton.

Restaurants opened up, and cruises up and down the river were a boom to the town. And a museum was opened up, too. There is one restaurant there that sells the best fish, while live fish swim around you in aquariums. Antique stores sprung up there as well. Several orchards were updated, expanded, and opened to sell fresh fruits and vegetables to the public. They have some of the best-tasting apples, strawberries, watermelons, and peaches you ever sank your teeth into. You can pick them yourselves or buy them by the peck, bushel, or pound. And now there are all kinds of weekend activities. Custom car shows, and historic, period rendezvous are held in the spring and fall. During these events the population of the city triples. People come from all over to reenact the meetings of the fur traders and Native Americans, who traded in furs, iron-made items, guns, black powder, and whiskey. There are cars lined up as far as the city limits of Alton. They are filled with tourists gawking and taking pictures. And after the flood, people built places for tourists to spend the night on weekend getaways. High upon the bluffs there is the most beautiful hotel and bed-and-breakfast establishments where one can go for a romantic weekend.

This was a sleepy little town that for the most part was ignoring strangers. But after the great flood, they took a new road on life. I always enjoy going there. I often take my family and friends there who are from out of town. They are always pleasantly surprised to go to a place thirty miles from Edwardsville (where I live) where they can see and do so many things for such a modest cost. This is a template for someone like you to show the residents how you and they can revitalize their town, provide jobs for the unemployed, and share the vibrant beauty of their piece of Americana. See, these ideas are ways the woman I started this talk about, and you too, can make your own steps in the new land that has opened up to you.

Readers Notes

It Doesn't Take a Lot of Talent To be Successful

WHEN YOU BEGIN TO CONSIDER WHAT YOU MIGHT BECOME in this new land, be original. Walking in steps made by others just will not make it. All the low-hanging fruit has already been picked. What is left is the choice fruit way up on the top branches. And let's face it, most of you are afraid of heights. And the rest of you can't climb very well either. So stay away from things already discovered and owned by someone else. I know of another fifty-year-old woman who wants to become an entrepreneur. Do not laugh, neither her age nor her being a female disqualifies her from living her dream. It is what she and many of you unconsciously do, that make your best and most sincere efforts failures. This woman wants to make it "big" by selling products from a vendor who sells through women's groups. The problem with this is she wants to hook her star to a pyramid scheme. What she and most people do not consider is that people are not paying premium prices for kitchenware anymore. Most of the younger generations are into cheap or inexpensive kitchen products that can be quickly replaced when they break, or if they are left behind, it doesn't matter. Along with this, the potential clients in her age bracket already have what she will be selling. She will need to search high and low for clients to make a success of her vision. I told her this and suggested she look at creating something novel to sell. Yes, she might come up with an original idea, product, or invention. A person doesn't have to be a genius to make it big. They just have to have sense enough to see a need going unmet and then create a product or service to fill the need. Most of you believe you need to have an IQ on the genius level. This isn't the case at all. Most of those who became successful entrepreneurs were average men and women. What each of them did was, they saw a need at the right time, and they supplied the solutions to that need. As long as many of you continue standing at the foot of the mountains, on this, the other side, you will have accomplished nothing. Come down and set your feet upon the new land and explore it. Always continue to remember that success rewards those who are prepared to receive it.

Preparation is the one key to success. One prepares by working hard and long at achieving the vision in his or her head. Granted there are cases of people with dumb luck. They back into a successful venture. Some inherit a fortune from some long-lost relative. They use the money to grow the original business, or they start additional ventures. Then there are those who hit it big by making mistakes that turn out to be groundbreaking advancements in science, economics, and business. These are the exceptions, not the norm. The majority of you will need to put your shoulders to the boulder and begin pushing it in the directions you want it to move. Here is where vision intersects with hard work to produce success. Let me share an example of what I mean. My son-in-law's sister married a most successful young man. He owns about a third of a chain of restaurants in an East Coast state, down South. This fellow wasn't born with a silver spoon in his mouth, either. In fact, he was homeless for most of his late teens and early twenties. Miraculously, he did not allow his circumstances to limit or impede his rise to the top. He could have turned to drugs and been another bum or vagrant on the streets. God knows every town and city has many a person who threw in the towel.

No, this young man had some innate, God-given drive within himself that compelled him to dream big dreams. He saw a vision of himself greater than his circumstances. He worked for one of those chain restaurants, of which he would eventually buy a third. Day in and day out he went to school, applied himself and took difficult courses. He took accounting, computer application courses, business law, and advanced language arts classes. Remember now, this he did while working at one of the stores he eventually bought. He did not have much time for girls, sports, and teenage antics. You see, when he finished serving the customers at the counters and cleaning up the place, he had to find a place to sleep for the night. Any other person might have lost it, but he didn't. This young man spent his breaks talking with the managers about how the business worked. He would come in on his off days to shadow them, so he could learn about just-in-time ordering of the merchandise. He learned how to project sales weeks in advance. He learned the importance of providing each customer with a quality product with a smile. He was not living at the level of his then circumstances. Instead, he was living the vision of what he would become. This man is now a multi-millionaire. His only talent was looking beyond where he was and seeing where he would be later on in his life. As you look out across the land, look for the place you want to be, and move judiciously in that direction. Let me share what this man did for my son-in-law.

My son-in-law attended a week-long training set up by the fellow. The guy was so gracious, inviting my daughter and their three kids to attend, as well. My son-in-law and daughter are becoming budding entrepreneurs. They have the makings of a great cheesecake pastry business. The business has gotten good press reviews, and it is growing in the Greater Peoria, Illinois, area. It was mentioned in the Peoria Journal Star for its great cheesecakes at the recent Taste of Peoria annual event. My daughter shared with me how the brother-in-law wanted the kids to attend, too. He knew they were working hard alongside their dad and mom, getting the business up and running. What a courteous thing for him to do. He is mentoring the adults and the children. His remarkable spirit is passing on to others what he discovered about how to become successful in life. I do know my grandchildren look upon their parents' business endeavor as theirs too. They spend time that the average boy or girl would waste, selling and delivering the cheesecakes. Perhaps they have already discovered that it does not take a lot of talent to be a success. It just takes vision and hard work to be successful.

 *Readers Notes*

The Land Allows You to Remake Yourself

JUST THINK OF THE HOMELESS MAN'S ACCOMPLISHMENTS. He rose from obscurity to prominence, wealth, and fame. In case you hadn't thought about it, once you climbed the mountains and made it onto the open land, you became changed individuals. You are no longer who you were on the other side of the mountains. You aren't even what you were becoming as you encountered dangers, risks, and temptations going through the mountains. You are metamorphic individuals. All you endured and went through has changed you. You are new creatures who have new insights on life. This means you are greater than what you were back then. You are also more than you imagined yourselves becoming. You were transformed mentally and physically as you struggled on your journeys. It is definitely true what they said about challenges building strength and character. You are part of an elite group. Nothing can slow nor stop you, but you. What you have to do now is learn how to enjoy the view of the open land. You see, so many people get so caught up in getting to a place. When they get to their destinations, they immediately turn around and return to wherever they came from in the first place. Remember, I touched upon people going back to the other side of the mountains earlier. They are almost never received well when they return with new knowledge and insights. Those who they tell about the other side of the mountains ask themselves, "If there is all that there, then why the hell are they here with us, so soon?" Believe me, this is a good question you need to ask yourselves. Leave the "dead enders" back where they are. Concentrate on you! Find for yourselves permanent places for you to fit into. Not all of you need to become captains of business. Some of you may choose to be healers, teachers, and guides for those who will come after you. For certain in these troubled times people could for sure use a steady voice to calm them. What you become, let it be your decisions. Do not allow others to use you to accomplish their goals.

Having lunch with my nephew and his son, we discussed how my older nephew, the father, was resisting being drawn into a codependent pit. His father and mother continue to pick up behind his other two brothers. They pay off their drug debts, and they tolerate the raging rants of the brothers when they are going through withdrawals from the drugs they are taking. He explained that his parents seem to think he should supplement their income to make up for what they gave, lost, and had stolen from his two other brothers. He was aware of his parents' attempts to place guilt upon him when he refuses to continue bailing them out. I concurred and agreed with his insight and decision. First, children are not to take care of parents who have their health and strength. One was expected to care for aging and ill parents, back in the day, but this is no longer done or expected culturally. Neither is a child expected to give money to support the illegal drug habits of his or her siblings.

I said to him that one cannot take care of dead weight people in his or her life. And I told him that he needed to expunge any guilt his parents or brothers wanted to lay onto his back. He agreed wholeheartedly with me. I shared with him how I too made the same decision concerning his family early in life. You cannot teach stupid people not to continue doing stupid things. Also, I wanted him to know you can acknowledge guilt, but cast from you shame. Shame is what people around you use to force you to conform to their ideas, thoughts, habits, and wishes. Remember, you left the other side of the mountains to get away from such an environment. And you for darn sure don't want to throw off one burden only to pick up another one like it in this new land. Burdens of external shame come between you becoming what God intended you to be. Shame stops you from doing what is needed to be done so you can become a better person. Your existence is for you to become what the universe, God, or your higher power wants you to become. It is not for you to spend your short lifetime being someone's physical and/or emotional slave. Be watchful and attentive of outsiders wanting to literally suck the life forces out of your being for their own benefit.

As my youngest nephew looked on and listened to the conversation his father and I had, I stopped and told him that life was shorter than he realized. I added, as a nineteen-year-old man, women would be looking for someone like him to take care of them, and they would not hesitate to get pregnant with his children to anchor him to them either. His father chimed in and shared how he sacrificed college to work and to take care of his mother, his siblings, and him, while his mother (the younger nephew's mother) stayed home. Yes, a sucker is still being born every minute of every hour of every single day of the week. My great-nephew is still looking at what he wants to become in life. He is like so many young men and women who have not decided what they want to start out doing and being in life. His father and I wanted to help him through the process. We did not want to decide this for him, but we also wanted him to be aware of the limitless possibilities available to him. We also told him of the thief of time itself, and how time was his most precious commodity. If he used it wisely, it would pay off with a high dividend for him.

Since meeting with my nephews, I have had my personal epiphany. Recently, another nephew invited me to take a seven-day cruise in the Caribbean with two of his female cousins and a large group from his church. He paid for me and the two cousins. We only had to provide for our transportation to and from Galveston. This was a wonderful gift for the three of us. We set sail mid-September. The wife did not wish to go, and besides she had just returned from a week-long road trip to Colorado. Well, let's just say I boarded the airplane at Lambert Airport as happy as a lark. The flight was an early bird one. We boarded around 6:30 a.m., and even then the plane was full. I got in line and eventually got a seat with one of my nieces because a very attractive woman graciously held the seat for me. I thanked her for being so thoughtful, and we made small talk.

Well, soon the woman started conversing with me while my niece sat between us. It soon became apparent that the woman was flirting with me. She poured out to me where she was coming from, and she managed to slip into the conversation that she lived in Key West. She even suggested I might want to move there and seek employment with the company for which she worked. I expressed my gratitude and politely declined her offer. I explained to her that I was retired, and had no intentions of re-entering the grid of clocking in and out. The conversation continued as we made our way to Dallas, where we switched planes. My niece saw what the woman was doing, and she blurted out, "Have you talked to aunt ..." She was signaling to the woman that I was married. This wasn't necessary because I was wearing my wedding ring. This upset me greatly, and I politely told my niece that I did not need her to run interference for me. I wasn't going to run off with the woman even if she was pretty. I further said to both nieces that I was old enough to take care of myself. And I was aware of my responsibilities too. I needed to put them in check, because so many people want to tell me, you, and anyone else, what they should or should not be doing. They were undone with me telling them to back off.

In life you too will need to speak up for yourselves. People who can't run their own lives feel it is their appointed duty to run yours. Nip this in the bud! While on the cruise more than a few attractive women flirted with me and I conversed with them and went on about enjoying my holiday. All this is to say, I am determined to live my life for me. I refuse to live it according to someone else's blueprint. You, too, have to do the same. We did not come down from the mountains to be led by outsiders. There were times when I was always behaving the way I thought others expected me to behave. Now, I couldn't care less about what they think of my behavior and actions. You and I only have to live by the internal locus of control that guides our actions and behaviors. Always remember, this is your life. And make darn sure you live it to the fullest extent. Never forget to live authentically during the time you have to live upon this world.

Readers Notes

Say What You Mean and Mean It

THE ROAD OF LIFE IS ACTUALLY THE PATHWAY YOU MAKE as you walk about the land. President Obama's second term as president has come to an end. Recently, he has been denigrated by foreign leaders at the G20 Conference in China. He is called an ineffective leader by the Republicans, racists and those who cannot give the man credit for what he accomplished during his two terms in office. What disturbs my train of thought is how President Obama allows people to insult him and this nation without obvious consequences. When you say here is the line and you better not cross it, mean it! I had hoped and prayed for President Obama to use his final months and days that remained in his administration to turn *The Audacity of Hope* into present realities. Unfortunately, he did not follow through. When the now President Trump began making a great deal of trash talk about what needed to be done, Obama should have stopped him. All he needed to do was to remind Trump that the country has only one president at a time. No, he allowed Trump to weaken his executive authority. All great leaders reminded the crowd who is the big dog in the room. President Obama never really did this. Leaders lead from the front. Authentic leaders from Abraham, Moses, Chaka Zulu, Abraham Lincoln, and Dr. Martin Luther King all heard what those around them were saying. But when decisions were finally made, they listened to the still quiet voice speaking to them deep within their souls. I say this because Obama seemed to listen too much to the women he surrounded himself with. Not to appear sexist, we now have a mess in the Middle East, the South China Sea, and in Ukraine. The only thing worse than what President Obama left to be cleaned up is for President Trump to make a bigger mess. Leaders listen to and they follow the voice spoken to them from within their souls and beings.

Abraham obeyed the voice that sent him on a foundational journey. He listened, and an old man and his old wife had a son who stretched forty-two generations in history to bring to the world Judaism and Christianity. Judaism gave the world the Ten Commandments and the brotherhood and sisterhood of all humanity. And it brought down the tyranny of Roman Power when a man called Paul gave the Roman world a new understanding of Judaism. Centuries later, a lean, unkempt lawyer from Springfield, Illinois, addressed the nation in his House Divided speech and won the office of president of the United States. He too was vilified by many, attempts were made upon his life, and from the time he left Springfield to occupy the White House until the assassin John Wilkes Booth approached Mr. Lincoln from behind and killed him. Perhaps knowing his time in life was short he listened to his inner voice. He signed into law the Emancipation Proclamation and rallied the Union to final victory over the Confederacy. He freed the Black men and women who were held for 349 years in slavery. He took the audacity of his dream and set the nation on a new course. Franklin D. Roosevelt, a crippled man, listened to his inner voice and took this nation through its greatest and longest economic depression, and almost to the ending that resulted in the defeat of Japan, Italy, and Germany in World

War II. When Mr. Obama listened to his inner voice and not to the voices of those around him he changed things. His vision became small glimmers of his realities. He led, and they followed. Even as he makes a new life for himself, post-White House, President Obama must not light a candle only to place it under a basket. I hope and pray that he remembers that a single light in the darkest of rooms, and times, drives away the darkness before it.

Hearing President Obama address the United Nations for his final time, he spoke clearly. He spoke with courage and he did not stammer the way he does at press conferences. Perhaps, in the past, before the press he felt guarded or afraid. When the press brought up questions about Black men and women being killed by police, he was very measured in his responses. He behaved similarly when he confronted Iran, China, and Russia. Maybe Mr. Obama did not want to anger China, Iran, or Russia while they openly challenged our Air Force and Navy. He is gone from office now, but I truly believe this was his weakest flaw. He did not use the power of his office to force his adversaries to back down. He did not listen to the voice of God telling what he needed to do, where he needed to be, and what he needed to say.

History shows that when tyrants make provocative movements they should and must be confronted. President Harry Truman did this when the Russians set up the blockade of West Germany. He fought the Communists to a draw in Korea. And he forced them into signing the ceasefire agreement by boldly placing the nuclear option on the table. I am aware of Mr. Obama's apparent inability to stand boldly in confrontational situations. He did not stand up to personal slights the way other Black men would do. Although I criticize him for this flaw, I feel this is due to him not being raised by a Black man. I am reminded that a child lives what he learns. And President Obama did and does not know that a "brother" does not let verbal or positional insults go unchallenged. This is not what is tolerated. Most Black men would rather lose their jobs than be denigrated publicly or privately by supervisors whom they view as incompetent and over-reaching. Case in point, Donald Trump's birth issue would not have gone on as long as it did if another Black man was the president then. All of this is to say to anyone listening, back up your words with judicious actions. On the basketball courts we call this taking names and kicking "A." The irony here is that President Obama was a good basketball player. Unfortunately, his moves on the court really did not transfer to the Oval Office. He always seemed conflicted.

I understand the risks of standing firm for one's convictions. It means you will sometimes lose the fight. But when the fighting is over, the other fellow will respect you because you opened up a can of hurt he too must nurse. Also, most rude, loud bullies are cowards who hide behind the crowd. They talk loudly and are harsh with their trash talking. But catch them alone, and they are different people. Let me share this story with you.

I was told a story of how Sen. Walter Mondale spoke out in opposition to a bill President Lyndon B. Johnson wanted passed. Senator Mondale ridiculed the president before the cameras and the press. But when a bill with appropriations for his state came before President Johnson, the president made a line-item veto of them. When Mondale came to the White House to protest, President Johnson dressed Mondale up and down. After being taken to the woodshed, Mondale never again disrespected the office of the president or the man serving in it. Donald Trump is now in the White House. You and I know he is not measuring what he says and how he projects himself. The man takes bold measures (right or wrong), and so far he has gotten away with most of his antics. Look at the two presidents and take the best of both. Use what you have taken, and do what it is that your inner voice tells you to do.

 *Readers Notes*

Be Prepared to Die for Your Core Beliefs

LOOKING BACK INTO HISTORY, I recall the great and final sermon given by Dr. Martin Luther King, Jr. He is someone that I look upon as saying what he meant and going to the point of dying for his convictions. Dr. King preached his own funeral in Memphis, Tennessee. He went down to Memphis to help the mostly Black sanitation workers. They were striking for living wages, and they were being treated inhumanely by the city. Dr. King was warned not to go to Memphis. He was told about plots against him. The plots were about people waiting to murder him if he went to Memphis. But Dr. King would not be dissuaded. Instead of listening to the warnings from those around him, he listened to the inner voice, telling him to go down to Memphis. He told the people at the church when he preached that he wanted to live a long life. And then he said, "I just want to be a drum major for justice." He finished preaching what has come to be known as his own funeral since he was assassinated by James Earl Ray the next day.

Most of us want to live long lives. Dr. King did, too, but he looked upon the injustices being perpetuated against the sanitation workers in Memphis as something needing to be confronted. I suspect being a theologian who received his dissertation in systematic theology, he read about men and women who gave their lives for divine truth. He saw in their words and deeds what it meant to speak truth to power. No doubt he read about Erasmus and Joan of Arc being burned at the stake for speaking out to power. He most surely read what Martin Niemoller wrote. Niemoller wrote, "First, they came for the communists and I did not speak out because I was not a communist. Then, they came for the socialists and I did not speak out because I was not a socialist. Then they came for the trade unionists and I did not speak out because I was not a trade unionist. Then they came for the Jews and I did not speak out because I was not a Jew. Then they came for me, and there was no one left to speak out for me." I am certain Dr. King went to Memphis prepared to give his life, if need be. He felt and saw that the sacrifice of one man could save the lives of many. Dr. King also knew the price of justice required each generation to pay it forward with the blood of the martyr. This has significant meaning in our present times.

As the nation and the world transition into the presidency of Donald Trump, there is much uncertainty. Are we allowing this man to extinguish the Lamp of Liberty? Will his accumulation of power move this great nation of ours into tyranny? There are parallels that look alarmingly similar to the movement that launched Adolph Hitler to the supreme leader of Germany, and the election of Trump to the White House. Just like Hitler, Trump was seen as a comic, a joke, but he disproved his critics. Hitler took the office of chancellor of Germany and within months imprisoned all who opposed him. Now, Trump is signing executive orders demanding federal workers stop sharing information with the press unless he gives permission. He unilaterally banned Muslims from entering the country, without seeking legal advice on whether this was constitutional or not. Hitler stripped the Jews of their German citizenship. Trump's band on Muslims kept Muslims with green cards from re-entering the nation after his executive order was issued. Hitler convinced the German people that they could defeat Soviet Russia within a matter of a few months. Trump is saber rattling against China over the territorial disputes in the South China Sea. He is threatening to march troops into Mexico without declaring war.

The German people followed Hitler and paid the ultimate price. Hitler got the German people in a war fought on three fronts. He could not defeat the combined forces of the British Empire, the Soviet Union, and the United States and its South Americans allies. Hitler was responsible for the deaths of 5 million German soldiers and sailors, 2 to 3 million civilians, and more than 20 million Soviet citizens and soldiers. The United States lost more than 131 thousand military personnel. Hitler's unchecked overreach led to the deaths of over 20 million people in Europe and North Africa. And after the war, his actions brought about the enslavement of millions of Eastern Europeans by the Soviet Union. If I am psychic, billions of lives may be lost if checks and balances are not placed on the antics of President Trump. Russia, formerly the Soviet Union, will re-enslave Eastern Europe.

Maya Angelou may be correct when she said, "The first time someone shows you who they are, believe them!" I feel in my gut that her words are correct when it comes to our current president. My mother and father had a similar saying, "Don't spend too much time listening to what a fellow says, just watch and see what he is doing." Ironically, the press and electronic media see President Trump lying and doing things he said he did not and would not do every day. It has been more than a year of seeing this man lying while people in charge are not calling him out for the liar he is. Is it going to take federal troops policing the streets of Chicago, and later, the streets of all the cities of the nation before someone realizes the threat to liberty this man poses? I feel the nation has entered a period when everybody wants to talk about "heaven", but "ain't" nobody willing to die to see that we get there. Too bad we don't have any spare Martin Luther Kings around. Looking down the road of tomorrow, I see many lives lost and tears shed. No one is brave enough to stand up and speak truth to power.

 *Readers Notes*

Follow Up Your Words with Action

ANCIENT HISTORY GIVES US AN EXCELLENT EXAMPLE of what saying and following up on your words can accomplish. Philip II of Macedon, Alexander the Great's father, conquered all of Greece with the exception of Sparta. Philip began making aggressive moves towards Sparta, and he sent Sparta a message saying what he would do to them if Macedon and Sparta went to war. Sparta's reply to the bellicose language of Philip was just one word, "if." Philip never again made threats towards Sparta. In fact, he left Sparta alone because he knew that Sparta was the one Greek city state prepared to fight and to resist Macedon until the death of the last warrior standing. And when the last Spartan warrior fell in battle, Philip knew he would have to contend against the Spartan women. Sparta had a history of saying what it meant and meaning what it said. In our modern times there are small nations who have stood up to vastly superior nations. Ninety miles off the coast of Florida, Communist Cuba has managed to remain the only Communist country in the Western Hemisphere. Fidel Castro and his small band of gorillas defeated the CIA-supported President Fulgencio Batista. Marxist or Socialist, Fidel Castro and his army defeated a dictator and made sweeping political and economic changes in Cuba. His reforms are debated by many here in the United States, but little Cuba has been independent since 1956. It is the only "Banana Republic" that has withstood the efforts of the CIA to topple it. Whether this is good or bad will be determined since full diplomatic relations have been reestablished between Cuba and the United States. What is does indicate is how one's words and firm resolve can overcome tremendous opposition.

To further make the point of saying and meaning, we only need to look at modern Israel and see the examples of what courageous efforts, hope, and audacity can accomplish. At the end of World War II, 6 million Jews had been murdered in Nazi concentration camps and by anti-Semitic people in the countries occupied by Nazi Germany. The Jews who remained found themselves unwanted throughout Europe. They were displaced people maltreated and without a home. Yet, they held on to the promise YHWH made to Abraham and his seed. Their national anthem entitled "The Hope" was sung in the displaced people camps throughout Eastern Europe. It was a song of hopeful promise that next year they would be in Jerusalem. The audacity of them to sing of this hope was insanity to those who continued oppressing them. But the Jews were determined to make Israel their home. The Jews living in Palestine and America redoubled their efforts to bring the Jews languishing in European camps to Palestine. In old, overcrowded, and leaking ships, Jewish refugees set sail for Palestine. The British did everything in their powers to dissuade them. The British turned back ships and imprisoned those they detained. They sent thousands back to their countries of origin, but the Jewish people returned again and again. Their ears were tuned to the promise YHWH made to Abraham and his seed. They drowned out the voices of disenchantment and discouragement, and they held on to their audacity of hoping for their own land.

The people would not be bullied, nor would they ever again be lambs led to the slaughter. There arose men and women freedom fighters who battled British occupation troops and Arabs who did not want large numbers of Jews in Palestine. The Jewish people were bent at times, but they refused to be broken. They fought for dignity. They fought for their existence, and they fought for the Land of Israel. Under the leadership of David Ben-Gurion, Israel became a modern state on May 14, 1948.

The Jewish ragtag band of freedom fighters drove the British out of Palestine. They also defeated the Arabs who violently opposed them in their hopes of establishing a Jewish homeland. Israel is now a sovereign nation, and for five decades Israel has held back the combined militaries of Syria, Egypt, and Jordan. The people of Israel have, additionally, confronted Iran, Saudi Arabia, and Iraq on the international stage for their continued existence. Eight to nine million Israeli Jews have and continue struggling and prevailing against the overwhelming weight of millions of Arabs and Muslims who want to see the nation of Israel wiped off the face of the earth. Today, Israel stands strong behind its "Iron Dome." Since returning to Palestine, Israel has made the desert bloom as the prophet Isaiah said (Isaiah 35:2).

Readers Notes

Time Goes by Fast
You Only Have a Short Time In It

MY NEIGHBORHOOD HAS GONE THROUGH SOME TURNOVER. Two turnovers have happened since we moved there more than ten years ago. We are seeing the second group of once babies now waiting to catch the bus to school. My wife, noting this fact, talked about how fast time goes by. We both understand the brevity of time and the life that goes with it. We only have a short time to live. When we were young we thought life would go on forever. As we age, we learn that there is not enough time in the day to accomplish all the things we have on our bucket list. And when we are still older, we come to understand that the time we have in life is as precious as money and its luxuries. The Sunday issue of *The New York Times* (September 11, 2016) had a most interesting article written by professors Hal E. Hershfield and Cassie Mogilner Holmes. Their article was entitled "More Time or Money? Your Choice." They discuss their findings written with a student named Uri Barnea. The team found that 64 percent of the 4,415 people they asked in five surveys valued money more than time. They also discovered the people who chose time over money were on average statistically happier and more satisfied with life than those who went for the money. They also noted that when additional income is needed to supplement income to cover living expenses, those who favored time took the money for short durations. The team concluded that people who chose time spent more of their time determining how they would spend their money. Their focuses were on what they wanted to spend money on and particularly on spending for needs. This is exactly what I discovered when I left the work world and retired.

Looking back over my six decades of living, I spent the majority of that time chasing after money. It was money to care for the family, money to keep the first wife happy, and money to keep up with the "Joneses." As you embark upon your journeys into the land try not to value money over time. The tragedy of many lives is they lived and died chasing after money. The vast majority of people you or I meet are consumed with purchasing the biggest house, the fastest car, and the latest fashion accessories. Then if they are suddenly without work or jobs, they scramble to take positions that supply the funds needed but often that are stressful and ill-suited for them mentally and/or physically. These types of jobs are killers. They give heart attacks, ulcers, chronic depression, hypertension, and death. Also the deaths they bring are often death to family relationships. As a pastor and chaplain, I rarely stood at the bedside of a person dying who regretted not making more money. Ninety-nine percent of the people talked of their wishes for more time. They wanted more time to say and to do things with their spouses, children, families and friends. Some who were dying expressed regrets about trips, vacations, and overseas adventures they never got around to making. The Bible says, "The lust for money is the root of all evil" (I Timothy 6:10). I have seen more people with huge sums of money tragically dying alone. What comes to my mind are the deaths of Michael Jackson and Prince; both of them left this world alone. Time is best spent with others whom you love.

You and I have seen people with little or no money who appear to be so happy. They are the ones who drive a ten-year-old van that is held together with duct tape. They sit in the free seats at the St. Louis Municipal Opera or in other venues in their cities. It doesn't matter to them if the family had to bring their own snacks with them. They are content to sit way back in the nosebleed seats because they can still see the actors on stage even if they are ever so tiny. What matters most to them is they are together as a family. And they are seeing a live stage performance. These folks have figured it out. Mom and Dad decided a long time ago that time spent together was more precious than that big new house. When the children came along, it was agreed that their care and education would be experiential. You can hear them saying, "Why look at a video on IMAX of the Grand Canyon, when we can see it live? Besides, we will see all the biomes and their life forms as we drive through the many states getting there." Unfortunately, many families give their children things and little else.

Should you walk through many American homes, you will notice how hurried everyone seems to be. There is constantly some place one or the other member in the family simply has to be. You notice they hardly ever sit down together eating. Often when they attempt this the television is on and their cell phones ring, disrupting any conversations that are taking place. Brevity is the decorum when they do sit down to eat. Eating together is a dash of fifteen minutes or less. And the majority of American families are so occupied with making money that breakfast is instant foods, and supper or dinner is carryout. This may be the norm, but I still like families that value time more than money.

More and more families are discarding things and downsizing. Tiny living is catching on with people. IKEA is serving this market, and entrepreneurs are building tiny houses that are 650 square feet or less in total living space. These are mostly young people who value time over money. They want more out of life than the accumulation of things. Besides, they know that you can't take things with you when you die. As wealthy as Ancient Egypt was, when the Pharaohs died and their tombs were sealed, thieves found ways to break into the tombs and steal their treasures. The families who value time spent with one another have learned it is the quality times that actually matter in life.

 *Readers Notes*

Regrets are Foolish Nostalgic Thoughts

I LOST A NIECE A FEW WEEKS AGO. She died after years of smoking cigarettes. The doctors told her that smoking was affecting her breathing. I know I was constantly on her about that deadly habit. For her smoking was truly an addiction. She just couldn't stop picking up a cigarette. Her death sent waves of reminiscence throughout the family. Some of the cousins and friends, too, felt they didn't do enough to stop her from smoking. It was wishful thinking on their parts because my niece was a grown woman. She made the decision not to stop smoking until it was way past the time to quit. She stopped when she only had 17 percent lung capacity. Her suffering was prolonged because neither she nor her cousins and other family members wanted her to give up on life. There were times when I felt she was ready to face death, but those around her bedside could not part with her passing from this life into death. I relate this to you because some members of the family have expressed their regrets. They speak as if there were things they could have done, but failed to do. As I said before, life is what we make of it. Her first cousin, who is experiencing complications due to so many mishaps, spoke to me about his feelings. He said, "If I could have been there, I could have helped her quit smoking." He felt he could have saved her. But I have come to see that the only person who can save you, is you.

Our lives are predicated on the choices we make. Some choices turn out well for us, and others do not. Regardless of the ones we make, we all live with the consequences that follow. I told my nephew this, and he wasn't listening to me. If one thinks too long and often he or she will not experience the here and the now. Depression will consume their thoughts and moments of joy and happiness around them will go unnoticed. The dark clouds of sentimentality were breaking up around his mind. Life and death are real, and relationships begin and they end. What matters when it all goes down, is what values we give to events and moments in time. In those moments of time when I get disappointed and discouraged, I think about what President Lincoln is purported to have said, "A fellow is about as happy as he makes up his mind to be." This sounds preposterous, outlandish, and silly. But I remember my mom talking about a man she would pass every day going to work. The man had no legs. Going to work and returning home, my mom saw the man sitting in the same spot. He was always singing and smiling even when it rained on him or was cold outside. She said the man taught her to look at each day as something to enjoy and to celebrate. I am not as consistent as the man was, but I have come to know that what Paul wrote to the Romans in the eighth chapter of that book in the New Testament is true. All things do work for good to them who have faith in God, the future, themselves, time, and tomorrow. As you go into the land, where you think you see barriers they will open up as you approach them. The only things between you and your destinies are the phantoms, the apparitions, and shades of the past.

Readers Notes

Place a High Premium on Yourself

YOU MADE IT TO THIS POINT because you felt, and you believed you were different from the people on the other side of the mountains. You even differentiated yourselves from the people you encountered getting through the mountains. You saw within your beings something that gave you the extra drive to persevere and not settle. You believed in you! This allowed great endurance to swell up within your beings. Now that you are traveling in the open land, you will need this same persistence. In other words, you must see yourselves as extraordinary. You are extraordinary individuals, and you should never forget this fact. To forget that you are special is to become nondescript, common, and ordinary. People who are average tend to cluster in the middle of the bell curve. You are at the other end of that curve. You are among those who are high achievers. Knowing this you need to always place a high premium on yourselves. Failing to do this will shortchange the images you want to project, and it will injure you economically as well as socially. I learned this the hard way, and I do not wish to see you spending half of your lives figuring out what I learned. Let me share some of my history.

I was born in St. Louis, Missouri, to a lower-class, African-American father and a mixed-race mother. She had Native

American and Black American heritage. My dad's grandmother on his father's side was redheaded with blue eyes. His mom was the most beautiful dark-complexioned woman you ever saw. My brothers and sisters run the entire color spectrum because we are all mixed up. Still, we were and are a close family who love and care for one another. Although we lived in public housing, my father and mother were determined to get us out of there. My parents only finished the eighth grade. Dad married Mom and inherited five stepchildren. They then had three more of us and adopted two boys they raised in foster care. My parents worked two, sometimes three, jobs to send an older brother and two sisters through college. They didn't have to tell me the importance of studying hard in school, so I could go off to college. It was a given to me. We lived in the projects, but the projects weren't in us. When I was in the eighth grade, the folks purchased a home in Alton, Illinois. My parents loved the place, but I hated it. It wasn't brand new. They did what so many other Black families were doing. They unknowingly financed new housing development for white people fleeing their new Black neighbors who purchased their old homes. Even at thirteen years of age I saw this, and I was determined to get the hell out of that house ASAP. That place was somebody else's dream. I graduated from high school and went off to college. It wasn't easy for me, but I moved through the classes and graduated. It took me five years to complete college, but I did finish. I worked full-time while in college. My parents were struggling to care for the grandchildren and the two younger boys. I worked to take some of the load off them. And I also worked to care for my new wife and son. I married at twenty-one during my senior year. I suppose getting married kind of pushed me into graduating. What I do realize is that I never allowed my circumstances to make me feel inferior or second rate. This attitude kept me hustling, going to the tutoring labs, until I graduated. I took an interest in being an ordained Christian minister and was blessed to receive a full scholarship from Eden Theological Seminary in St. Louis, Missouri. I also took an extra year to finish there. To this day I send the seminary a little money because they took a chance on me when they did not have to do so.

By the time I decided to pursue an MBA, I had learned how to study and how to think. I managed to graduate with honors. I share all this to say that I valued who I was. I did not allow my environment to determine the boundaries of my accomplishments. Even when a racist Italian history teacher told me I wasn't smart enough to get into graduate school, let alone graduate, this did not deter me. I knew that I was going to accomplish everything I set out to conqueror. I looked upon myself as being a premium being. I refused to allow roadblocks to become permanent barriers. Study the situation when things do not work out as they should. There are always ways of achieving your objectives and, eventually, your goals. More importantly, I eventually learned not to sell myself too cheaply.

During my years as a Christian minister I always found myself in dying and struggling congregations. I would get them up on their feet and be sent by the bishop off to another and another appointment just as bad, or in worse condition, than the last one I pastored. Finally, I had an eye-opening moment. I was settling for things below my pay grade. I endured a divorce during my years as a pastor. I also spent thirteen years as a public school teacher before I refused to settle anymore. I share all of this because I hope you will not wait too long before realizing the worth you bring to any situation. I want to share what I did when the exact same scenario presented itself to me later on in life.

The Baptist Church my parents were members of was facing a crisis. Their long-serving pastor died. The congregation brushed aside my application for the pastorate. They called another man to succeed their deceased pastor. He was singled out and chosen by a few of the deacons and trustees who heard him preach when they visited his congregation in Texas. The fellow lacked seminary training, while I did have seminary training. He could sing and preach like the old-time preachers did back in the day. I could not sing in the shower. And the members were uneasy about my divorce and my leaving the Methodist Church. I had my warts and all, but in addition to seminary training I had over thirteen successful years as a pastor. I was also a certified teacher in grades K through 12 and held administrative certification as a chief school business official. This did not matter to them. They looked over me. And before I forget it, I also held an MBA. But nothing seemed to impress the church.

They called and elected the man from Texas. He was nothing like the gentle, long-serving pastor that died. The first sermon or two the fellow preached, he used a broom to exorcise or to symbolically demonstrate to the deacons and trustees that he was the anointed king and head authority of that church. He then proceeded to take over every committee in the church. He ruled the people as if he were Ivan the Terrible. The deacons and trustees were shocked, and they acted as if they were powerless to deter the man. This went on for five or more years. The financial surplus was depleted, and the members did what Baptists always do, they voted with their feet. They began staying home or they began attending and joining other congregations. The straw that broke the camel's back was when the man attempted to seduce a married woman who belonged to the congregation. With stealth, the deacons and trustees managed to terminate the man. Their timing couldn't have been worse because they fired their pastor when he was in the hospital having a leg amputated due to diabetes complications. This caused half of those who were still faithful attendees to stay away from the church. It came to the point when there were sometimes more people in the choir singing than there were sitting in the pews. Where there once were three hundred to four hundred people attending worship on a good Sunday, now just a small percentage showed up for worship. Weeks went by with empty pews.

When the money to pay the bills was depleted, the deacons and trustees decided to take drastic actions. They called me and asked me to preach. I had been given privileged information alerting me that I was their candidate of last resorts. The majority of the deacons and trustees were ecstatic over the prospects of me succeeding their former pastor. But I was in a different place by then. When I was ready and willing to become their pastor, they overlooked me. You see, I was exhausted, tired of being a turnaround pastor. My accomplishments were never followed by any significant increases in salary. Now, I just did not want to return to what was a major factor in my divorce. Perhaps my ego got in the way too. But when they entertained me as worthy of becoming their pastor, I was retiring from my secular job as a teacher. I was ready to retire, and I did not want to retire from one job only to immediately take on another job. I'd worked from the time I was eight years old. Besides, I remembered saying years earlier to my older brother who was a pastor, "I hope when I get old, I have sense enough to know when to retire." He was well past sixty-five and fighting with his bishop, who wanted to relieve him of his long-running position of presiding elder in the

African Methodist Church. My words came back to haunt me. How could I do what I berated my older brother for doing? But still, the church was in serious trouble.

Black churches are dying now, just like white churches have been doing. Feeling remorseful for the church, I signaled to the interim pastor and to several of the deacons and trustees that I would serve for six months. I proposed that during the six months, I would work to foster healing and to bring the congregation back together. I would also make the congregation financially solvent again. I knew I could do this. During my thirteen years as a mainline pastor, I turned dying congregations around. Several years earlier I had proven to the community what I could do. When I returned to the area, I took over the reins of another church. It had been three former African Methodist congregations who broke away to become one larger united body. They had problems coming together. There were issues of direction, trust, and power, but still I took the position and transformed the three feuding bodies into one strong and cohesive church. Allow me to share this triumph.

Unity Fellowship Church was struggling to become a real church. It was floundering for about five or six years. Before calling me to get them together, they stepped over me and called a young man to be their pastor. He had recently graduated from seminary. Unfortunately, he preached and pastored there two weeks before he took seriously ill and died. Then I was their go-to guy. I was eventually given the pastorate and immediately went to work. With faith and determination, I got them out of a rented hall that leaked profusely every time it rained. They had been there for five years. Then, I led them in the purchasing of a nearly new church building and grounds which were for sale. The properties belonged to a Reformed Congregational Church that disbanded. The disbanded congregation just could not make it after the founding pastor left. They were down to two dozen members, and they wanted to sell the building and 2.1 acres of land for just $220,000. They even threw in the old parsonage with the deal. The sanctuary was just five years old and in excellent condition. The congregation and I purchased the building and grounds and retired $110,000 of the indebtedness that first year. Additional updates and improvements were undertaken. Tired of the bickering that began anew over little, silly things, I left after that first year as pastor. Before leaving I succeeded in helping the congregation find my replacement. Their new pastor was even better than I was on paper. He was seminary trained and possessed his Ph.D. in Education Administration. Digressing, the Baptist Church that was in serious trouble had a recent reference of my capabilities. I was capable, willing, and ready to assist my parent's old church in getting back on their feet. But things did not turn out as I had hoped.

When I preached on the appointed Sunday asked of me, I made it clear to those in worship that I was retired and not interested in returning to full-time service in the ministry. I also shared my availability for six months to prepare them to know what they wanted in their next pastor. And I outlined how I would help them to bring about healing within the congregation. Additionally, I promised that during the six months I would get them in financial shape that would allow them to flourish once again. After that, I preached the morning sermon and I left. The deacons and trustees did not receive my proposition or the sermon well. The congregation of fifteen or more souls in attendance wanted me to preach a fire-and-brimstone sermon. This I did not do. Instead, I preached taking hold of the gospel plow and not looking back. You would have thought I possessed some pre-cognition feelings or ideas about what that day would be like with the congregation. All during the liturgy the interim pastor and the deacons talked about their deceased, long-serving pastor. They reminisced about the "good old days" and times when the pews were filled with worshipers. I wanted them to understand that what is behind them was lost, gone, and dead. What was before them was their future and a new beginning. The sermon and its message were not well-received. You see, they wanted to return to the good old days. But they failed to remember what their last search for a pastor had done to the church and what it continued doing to the church. Even with the latest pastor gone, they needed to tidy some things up. Reconciliation needed to be made between the factions in the church. My message to them that day fell on deaf ears. They ended communications with me after this. They are still without a pastor, and things do not look promising for their continued existence. You might feel I short-circuited the process. I may have done just that, but I did what I did. Yes, there was a high probability of me becoming the pastor of that church. I would have had extra income coming in to boost my retirement income. But to allow the process to play out the way they planned was no longer a good fit for me. Within me a radically transformative change had taken place. I offered them a bargain, but they refused the deal. My negotiating style is to first offer a win/win proposal. I saw, and continue to view myself as a vetted, seasoned, turnaround pastor. I wish them well as they search for a pastor to guide them. As for me, I refuse to allow another congregation or denomination to tell me I have to take what they offer me without question.

You may be asking yourselves if I realized that I lost out on a job opportunity. Yes, for certain the earning potential went down the drain. But I gained even more by breaking away from an old habit. I may have crossed my mountains and in some ways walked on the open land. But deep within me my spirit was still on the other side of the mountains. I continued to instinctively want to do what I had always done, that is until this situation. When I proposed to the congregation my planned agenda for revitalizing their failing situation, I became the primary actor and not the reactor in my life and for my life. This brought about a tremendous shift in my psyche as well. I suddenly saw myself as more than a pastor who was also an educator. When you look on the face of both of my former professions, they were actually one and the same. I left teaching religious subjects only to begin teaching secular ones. During that process, I saw and heard from deep within my being a voice urging me to write. The voice seemed to compel me to share my journey through the mountains. So in a way, the land opened up to me the opportunity to share the sum of my life experiences. All I needed to do was to understand that most of the people in the world are on the other side of the mountains. And some of the people are up in the mountains. Then there are some in a suspended environment on the other side of the mountains where the land opens up. I was in the last group.

I made it through the mountains, but psychologically and physically, I was just standing and looking off into the distance. I had not emotionally or physically set foot on the open land. I kept doing things that psychologically drew me back to the people I left on the far side of the mountains. My enticements were going into the ordained ministry and after that becoming an educator. My last temptation was the opportunity to become the pastor of the church, a position I had once coveted and wanted so badly. Then suddenly I listened to the still silent voice speaking out from the depths of my soul. The voice compels me to write. It is as if a hidden spring bubbled up from within. The spring wanted me to know that authentic living is not working for a salary on a job in a profession that gives you the economic resources to purchase more and more things. You and I got through the mountains to partake of the experiences that awaited us in the open land. How much money we can make or the square footage of the big houses we can purchase is not what authentic living is all about. Those things are traps and glitches playing ring around the roses. I no longer wanted to play this game until the day I died. There is something greater than living to acquire things. Real living is much more than these anomalies. You and I have seen so many things in life. We now have an understanding of the intrinsic, spiritual dimensions of live.

We understand without knowing why things in and of themselves are poor stand-ins, understudies, and substitutes for learning the meaning of life itself. Like the Buddha we looked for nirvana, enlightenment, bliss, joy, paradise, and heaven, high and low. When we did find peace or shalom, it was ours when we listened to the voice of the universe. The voice was not outside of us. The voice spoke to us from within. The voice came to us in many forms. To some it was YHWH, Jesus, or Allah speaking. We were urged to walk faithfully through the open land. We were given the assurance that along the way whatever we needed would be provided. I have learned through experience that God will provide for my every need. You and I are *qadash*, or set apart for the service of God. Our gifts come with great responsibility. We are voices crying out for justice and righteousness. Everywhere we look there is chaos, death, violence, and upheaval. Here in America we have government that does not work. We have racism, large numbers of people poor, or nearly poor, and out of work. Police are unjustly killing Black men and other ethnic minorities. Then there are civilians killing police in a tit for tat game of death. And don't get me started on the international issues.

Irish philosopher Edmund Burke wrote, "The only thing necessary for the triumph of evil is for good men to do nothing." We were called to be agents of positive change. This charge is an extremely important one. Our voices are sometimes drowned out by the noises of idiot cable television and radio. These mediums dull the senses of the billions. They parley the propaganda of the corporate elites. Their propaganda demands the masses offer more and more of their flesh and blood to the fertility gods of consumerism. On the other side of the mountains and here on the open land, our mission is to show humanity how to live with nature instead of destroying nature. This is nothing new—life is cyclical, recurring, repeated phases. Now is the time to reset the phase back to its humane setting. Moses gave the Hebrews the Torah which showed the people how to be stewards of the land. Yu the Great, the legendary first Emperor of ancient China, gave the people the technology to control the waters of the great rivers. Thus, the people ate from the bounty of the soil. Others in countless cultures rose up and aided the people in the pursuit of living within nature. They were as you are today, lights pushing aside the darkness. So move out from where you are and spread out onto the open land. And never doubt that you are special and unique.

⊢━•⊙•━┤ *Readers Notes* ⊢━•⊙•━┤

You Cannot Change Stupid

SEVERAL DAYS AGO I attended a meeting of the homeowners' association that oversees the subdivision in which I live. In attendance was a young yuppie couple. This couple craved the attention of the others. On more than one instance during the meeting they brought up that they had just completed a costly renovation in the backyard of their property. I could look and see that they were annoying the others there and me as well. They went on about how they had increased their property value. But they wanted to protest the association's prohibition against above-ground swimming pools. This couple wanted to play the semantics game of what constituted an above-ground pool. According to them the inflatable pool they had and used for two months out of the year wasn't actually an above-ground swimming pool. This went on and on, they even brought up the issue of little kiddie pools. You know the ones parents purchase at the dollar store or at Walmart. You may have seen infants splashing while their mom and dad cool them off on a hot summer day. The elected board explained to them that these weren't the kind of above-ground pools that were permanently set up. They explained to the couple that once the parents had finished, the water was poured out and the pools were put away. The pair wasn't buying this explanation. Finally after thirty minutes of listening to the pair, a board member spoke up and said, "According to the manufacture of your pool, it is listed as an above-ground pool." The guy had looked up the company that made the pool. He had the specs and photos of the pool, too. Do you think this settled the matter? No, it did not settle the matter. By this time I had had enough of going around and around in circles. So I motioned for the meeting to be adjourned and got a second on the motion. The voice vote was taken, and those in favor of the motion prevailed.

All of this nonsense moved me to affirm, you cannot fix stupid. The vast majority of the unenlightened members of society will spend their entire lives without turning on the light bulbs hanging over their heads. These are the ones who proverbially cannot see the forest for the trees. When you look at the two candidates who ran for president, you shake your heads. One of the candidates was and is unstable, a bold-faced liar, a narcissistic self-centered reincarnation of Stalin or Adolf Hitler. This guy looks into the camera and lies. When confronted about the lies he told and continues to tell, he calls his confronters liars. And the people committed to him make excuses for him, and they get into lock step behind him. Are we in a George Orwell, 1984, moment? Only stupid people vote for a "demigod" who has always burnt those who dealt with him in the pass. The leopard never changes is spots. He uses them to camouflage himself into the surroundings as he awaits his prey. The people following the man elected president can't see that it is they who are the prey. Heaven help them and the rest of us. We have four years of this man being president of the United States. I only hope we are still united when the four years are up. I continue to believe a person's past actions are his or her record of behavior. One's behavior patterns are not readily changed unless there are divine internal interventions, or outside ones. Up to this point in life I do not see any major shifts in the behavior and actions of the guy we just elected president of the United States.

Then there is the other candidate. She is perceived by the above person's followers as being the biggest liar of all time. Looking over her track record leads one to believe that she has more lapses of judgment than being a liar. How in the world would a person serving the nation as secretary of state install and use a private, unencrypted server in her home to carry out the official business of that office? And how could she not think of the risks of cyber attackers reading everything she composes in real time? This person graduated with a juris doctorate from Harvard University. You would expect someone as intelligent as her to have known better. As with her and the other guy, you cannot fix, alter, or change stupid. Looking at the political process that ushered these two to the forefront, one can only exclaim how stupid the election process is. Know that stupidity cannot be changed. Perhaps it is time for "we" the more level-headed thinkers to abandon the current election process. It needs to be replaced with another, better one, at all deliberate speed. The problem with being stupid and following stupid leaders is thatit makes you stupider than those leading you.

⊢━━•◉•━┥ *Readers Notes* ⊢━━•◉•━┥

All the Wealth You Acquire Stays Here When You Die

SEVERAL DAYS AGO, I READ AN ARTICLE ONLINE listing eight men who have more wealth than 3.6 billion people living at the bottom of the economic ladder. It was CNN news that shared this startling information. Eight humans added together hold such enormous wealth. Staggering should be the word that comes to mind when you think about the disproportionate way the wealth to humans is computed. Let us look at this equation seriously. The current population of the world is 7.5 billion people (www.worldometers.info/world-population). Take 3.6 billion and divide it by 7.5 billion and it means that nearly half of the world's wealth (.48) is in the hands of just eight men. This is insanity at its worse. How can the world continue to allow such inequality to exist? The answer is because the masses of the people are either kept in subjugation by oppressive governments or in the so-called democracies, the masses are pitted against one another. Here in the United States it is the Alt-Right, and other white supremacy groups, fighting Blacks and other colored ethnic groups over non-intrinsic things, like skin color. The white groups run the systems that bar Muslims from entering the country until they are vetted. They cheer the news that says there will be a wall built separating Mexico and the United States. They become rapturous when told Mexico will pay for the wall. What they do not see is that the wall will be paid for through increased costs added onto goods and services coming into the United States from Mexico. And as for the Muslim ban, vetting any and all foreigners entering the country is needed and important. It is not safe for people to enter the country without notification. They could be agent-provocateurs who are sent from foreign countries.

However, I am mindful of the turning away of the MS St. Louis in 1939. On board that vessel were Jewish refugees trying to escape the genocidal "final solution" of Adolf Hitler. Historians have estimated that approximately a quarter of them perished in the concentration camps. I just hope and pray history will not be repeating itself when it comes to Muslims fleeing their war-torn countries. As for the longest oppression of a minority group, give or take another two or three generations, Black Americans will cease to exist as an authentic entity. Black Americans make up 13 percent of the United States population. But they comprise 48 percent of the prison population. In real figures, this is an astonishing 2.2 million Blacks locked up (http.www.laprogressove.com//black-men-prison-system).

If you seek to destroy a people, break the family structure down. Kill its men outright, and if you cannot do this, render them physically and psychologically neutered. The television commercials urging people to adopt children is the government seeking placement for the thousands of Black children in foster care. The dysfunctional Black family structure is unable to replace itself with stable homes where there are married men and women living together. It still takes strong Black men to raise strong Black boys and girls into adulthood. Black women are overworked trying to do this and many are giving up the struggle. Those who are continuing the work are losing their sons and daughters to drugs, HIV-AIDS, and drive-by shootings. Then there is the unspoken matter of Black men going into prison and coming out of prison as practicing bisexuals. This is learned behavior, and it is destroying the segment of Black America that is in its child-bearing stages. How is this destruction done? It is done with babies born HIV positive: It is done when ex-convicts cannot find gainful employment. It is done when more and more men are chasing other men instead of women. This phenomenon has given rise to Black women becoming "switch hitters" themselves. This is the national norm among Blacks in America. Think I am lying? Just read some of the Facebook pages of Black Americans.

Poverty is the condition of most Black Americans. Their poverty is so deep that it has taken from the vast majority the will, the ability, and the knowledge of how to lift one's self up by his or her boot straps. Masses of Black Americans are hopeless, dying, and cannot seem to figure out ways to stop their downward spiral. But what the Alt-Right and other white supremacy groups neglect to realize is they are experiencing similar problems with their ranks. Opiate drug addiction is at epidemic proportions in their homogeneous communities. It is not the Blacks and Hispanic "thugs" that bring these drugs into urban and rural America. It is other whites doing this. And it seems that the diseases and pathologies that are destroying Black society have now begun attacking white society. Rural and urban Americans have been ravaged by the exportation of good-paying jobs to other countries. Globalization, as coined by the late Peter Drucker, is the economic system that purports to raise the levels of all national economic systems at the same time.

Globalization in theory sounded great. Production would always flow to the countries that could produce or provide services at the lowest cost. But in actuality the financiers began a race to the bottom with nations bidding to produce and manufacture things lower than their actual cost of production. It has left the United States with rust-belt cities. America no longer makes the steel. It's no longer in the business of making cell phones, computers, and televisions. Even the clothing on the racks of the nation's department stores is not made in America anymore. Global companies make these things cheaply and sell them in America for lower prices than they would usually cost. But who can purchase a silk suit for $100 if you do not have that amount between all the working folks in your household? It is as if the economy is a dish rag that was once wet and full of dish water. Now it has been squeezed so tightly, until the rag isn't even damp anymore.

This is what the Alt-Right and the others who still view the world through the eyes of skin color should notice. The rich and the super-rich no longer look at the world through nationalistic eyes. They look at the world as a place where their corporations can make large profits while paying their workforces the lowest possible wages. Supreme Court Justice John Roberts said corporations were no longer "ongoing concerns." He and the majority of the court see corporations as "people." And we all know the big fish always gobbles up the little fish. Eight men hold 3.6 billion dollars in their hands. People are starving and dying all over the world. The world faces climate change. Air pollution is taking the lives of people in China, India, and even Poland. With three-fourths of the surface of the earth covered in water, we are facing shortages of clean drinking water throughout the world. Just look at the travesty that has taken place in Flint, Michigan. Perhaps an entire generation of that city's youth will not be capable of being productive Americans because the governor and his appointees elected not to treat the water system for lead poisoning. To them, such prudent actions were not cost effective.

It is good to have enough money to purchase food, clothing, and to do some of the things you and the family want to do together. But how much is too much money? It remains to be seen when one considers the super-rich still have not come to see that when they breathe their last breaths, the money stays here. I just hope they will understand this and become today's Andrew Carnegies. Mr. Carnegie made billions of dollars by today's standards. After he acquired huge sums of money, he gave much of it away. In fact, Andrew Carnegie gave away 90 percent of his wealth. He built 2000 libraries across America (I am sitting in one of the libraries that his generosity made possible). He founded the Carnegie Institution to fund scientific research and to establish a pension system for public school teachers. Last, he gave money to build The Hague Palace of Peace in the Netherlands. He was a man who believed in the Gospel of Wealth. He knew … "to him who is given much, much is required" (Luke 12:48).

Readers Notes

There Will be Many Twists and Turns
They Will Eventually End
Where You Should Be

LIFE IS LIKE RIDING A BUS. You get on and off when you make transfers. Each and every transfer gets you closer and closer to your destinations. Be aware of this as you move to fulfill your callings. Not one single change agent went immediately from point A to point B. It does not happen that way. Changing systems, people's thoughts, and accomplishing what you set out to do are filled with twists and changes. I am again reminded of Dr. Martin Luther King, Jr., and what he went through to witness President Lyndon B. Johnson signing the Civil Rights Bill. Martin was stabbed by a deranged, unbalanced woman, and he nearly died from this injury. He was imprisoned many times for calling upon the nation to live up to its credo, beliefs, and principles. His house was bombed, frightening his wife and children who were inside. He went to Memphis, Tennessee, to support the sanitation workers who were predominately Blacks, and he was assassinated at the Lorraine Motel. The stops Dr. King made along his journey did not end his dream. The final stop at the Lorraine Motel ended his mortal life. The bullet killed his body, but still his dream is alive. Dr. King's words continue to echo from the void of time and space themselves. Truth and justice can be slowed, but they will eventually get you to the place where you should be.

The night before Dr. King became a martyr, the sanctuary was packed. People were standing along the walls and anywhere else they could. Dr. King wanted to shore up the courage of the people there. You see, there was a court injunction against the strikers and the marchers. On that night Dr. King rose up last to speak to the people in that time of great anxiety. He talked about the storm that had been forecast for that evening and how the people disregarded their safety to be at the service that night. And Martin said there was another kind of storm coming in Memphis.

Martin proceeded to address the gathered people there in his eloquent style of Baptist preaching. He used the cadence of his voice to take the people on an imaginary journey through time itself. He began in Egypt and he took the listeners to Ancient Greece. There Martin and the people took stops during the many periods of perilous times and the triumphs that prevailed in each of those situations. One thing Dr. King said that remains etched within me was that, "No longer is there the choice between violence and nonviolence. It is [now] nonviolence or nonexistence." He continued on by stirring the courage and the hope of the people by telling them, "Only when it is dark enough can you see the stars." He went on to remind the people of their agenda: unity against injustice. He spoke for nearly fifty minutes without manuscript and as the culmination of his address, he told them, "I have been to the mountaintop." He then told the people there of his wanting to live a long life, but he also added, "I just want to do God's will."

Dr. King had a precognition of his impending assassination. If he did indeed know he was going to die soon, it was there that he connected with his transfer point. The bus they were traveling on that night would take the rest of them back home to their own different destinations. Some, like Dr. King, did not make it to the Promised Land. But they, too, were allowed to view from afar the Promised Land. Young people and children such as I, were also allowed to enter the Promised Land. We crossed our Jordan River and marched around until Jericho's wall of overt racism and out-and-out sexism came tumbling down. But we now contend against a form of racism that has changed its name. Still it is the same old poison that kills and destroys. Dr. King, at his last sermon in Memphis, began addressing the demon named economic injustice. He knew that a society, a civilization, a world cannot exist where 99 percent of the populace are have-nots. He knew that in a land where great medical advancements abound, but these advances are only for those with the ability to pay, this was incipiently evil. Dr. King knew this land was moving closer and closer to the loss of its empathy and its ability to care for the least of God's children.

Dr. King viewed the worst that could befall humanity from the mountaintop, but he also saw what justice herself would bring about. He knew the universe, however long it takes, makes things right. You and I are all passengers on this bus. We get on the bus at certain stops along the route. As we travel we transfer to other buses and take other routes. But those of us who have lived awhile, we have learned that the buses all end up taking their passengers to same place. We all eventually end up at the terminal where each one of us learns that the final destination wasn't the point. What actually mattered was the journey itself. Looking at the lives of those who got through the mountains and then entered into the land, one sees individuals who looked at the things along their paths. Life is not getting to one place or another. Life is the journey itself. We all are born, we live, and eventually we die. The tragedy of so many of us is that we never take notice of the things and people we pass along the way. While in the mountains, you have seen or will see the Promised Land. When you descended the mountains and made your way onto the open land, you left your footprints there. Hopefully, you did more good than bad. Prayerfully, you forgave more than you cursed. Thankfully, you accepted acts of kindness from strangers, and you gave the same to others whom you met along the way.

Finally, for those of you whose buses have arrived at the bus terminal, you can look back over your uprisings and down falling and not complain. You and I know the journey is itself sanctification of our souls. When we have reached our end point, we return to the Creator who gave us the visions to leave the others on the other side of the mountains. Coming behind us are others who will hear the call when the time is right. They too have to make the same journey. Like us each one of them will finish the journey in his or her own unique and special way. In all good time, and with prayerful hope, they too will make it to the end point of human existence. Hopefully, they too will have discovered that the meaning of life is living life the way God intended for each of us to live it.

━━•◦•━━ *Readers Notes* ━━•◦•━━

Closing Thoughts

As I come to the end of this discussion, hopefully you have come to understand that the journey is to find self-actualization. We learn the good from the bad. We become set apart to call the world to right living. We offer alternatives to the destructive forces and institutions in life. Always remember that the journey does not begin when one physically heads towards the mountains. It starts when people come to the decision that they can no longer exist as they currently are. The sojourner then begins making preparations to emotionally and physically separate from the collective. This is where people abandon all they know, all they have been taught, and begin the process of becoming individuals. For the first time in life each of these individuals stands alone and against the mass of others. This is frightening and yet freeing for the man or woman who begins looking at what is on the other side of the mountains. He or she knows of the perceptions of how others view him or her. When a person leaves the familiar and goes off in search of self, he or she is as a child exploring the environment for the first time. New realities are discovered and experienced. Most important to the sojourner is knowing each obstacle conquered is an affirmation of his or her decision to leave the familiar behind. Whenever a child learns a new skill that child increases the reach of his or her environment. If you do this, you will be like this child. In the mountains you are made to do things you have never done before. Each new encounter drives you on to the next, and you come to see that you are capable of living without the assistance of those whom you left behind. You meet new people, learn about new cultures, new ideas, and the shortcomings of each of them. Your clearer understanding forces you to move on towards the other side of the mountains.

Some people make it through the mountains to the land that opens up rather quickly. They are driven to quicken their tempo so they can find and explore the other side of the mountains. These are often the very young. The young haven't had as much indoctrination as the older adults from the collective. Still, they must be careful not to trade one group of oppressors for another that is just as oppressive and destructive as the one left behind. Those who are older and more mature have implanted within their minds schemas of what worked back on the other side of the mountains. For them to be successful, most of what they learned on the other side of the mountains has to be cast aside. They have to extrapolate and devise new adaptations to their new environments on the other side of the mountains.

You have the very young seekers and the older, more mature seekers. Each group has its strengths and its weaknesses. Ideally, the two groups will come together and network and give mutual aid and protection. They must be cautious in not forming as rigid a structure as the one they left behind. They have to remember that it was freedom of thought, ideas, and exploration that drove them to traverse the mountains and move on to the land. Once on the land, they are as newly hatched chicks or baby turtles. Around them on the open land there are predators who gobble up the unsuspecting. Vigilance is what has to be observed from this point on. Yes, in the mountains they had to look out for the dangers nature presented to them. But in the open land, other humans are more dangerous than anything they will encounter in life. When the individuals make it onto the open land, they must begin discovering it; discovering who they are. Some spend lifetimes finding who they are and what purposes they were made to accomplish. Others come to understand their purposes in life rather quickly. What is important is they come to the freeing of self-actualization or finding their fullest potential. Let me share examples of people who have completed their journeys through the mountains. Here below are some people who have found themselves.

When you read and see on the news stories of transgender people affirming themselves you are looking at and reading about a group of people beginning their journey through the mountains. These men and women are demanding the collective to allow every man and woman the freedom and the rights to become what the universe has called him or her to be. When you look at the millions of Middle Eastern men, women, and children, crossing oceans, seas, mountains, while armed factions are killing each other, and those journeying with them, you are looking at travelers. They left their ancient lands seeking safety, the freedom of their beings and the re-invention of their lives. When you see Black and Native Americans marching and protesting for their right to live in liberty, freedom, and without fearing for their lives, you see individuals who have come together for their general needs. Black lives matter, and the rights of Native Americans should matter enough for federal and state governments to give them equal protection under the law. These groups are not waiting for the above to take actions. They are prime movers of their individual and collective agendas.

There are others who have left the mountains, and who have moved onto the land. Each is an individual who struck out on his or her own to discover why he or she was born. As a collective group, they want to know their purposes in life. They leave the stifling of the other side of the mountains and begin the journey because they know life has more to offer than the confinement of the ordinary. Hopefully, you will begin your own journey. Some of you are already in the mountains. You are doing everything you can to make it through the mountains. You want be what God wants you to be. Keep going and do not stop. Keep going and do not look back. One thing I do know is, once you get through the mountains, the land does indeed open up.

 *Readers Notes*

Acknowledgements

Special thanks to my brother Reginald, my nephew Jeff, and to my publisher, Ted Parkhurst, the man who made a special trip to Edwardsville to encourage me in my writing.